Other books by Debra K. Farrington

Hearing with the Heart: A Gentle Guide for Discerning God's Will for Your Life

Living Faith Day by Day: How the Sacred Rules of Monastic Traditions Can Help You Live Spiritually in the Modern World

One Like Jesus: Conversations on the Single Life

Romancing the Holy: Gateways to Christian Experience

Unceasing Prayer: A Beginner's Guide

Learning
to Hear
with the Heart

Meditations for Discerning God's Will

Debra K. Farrington

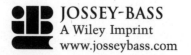

JOSSEY-BASS
A Wiley Imprint
www.josseybass.com

Published by Jossey-Bass
A Wiley Imprint
989 Market Street, San Francisco, CA 94103-1741   www.josseybass.com

Jossey-Bass books and products are available through most bookstores. To contact Jossey-
Bass directly call our Customer Care Department within the U.S. at 800-956-7739, outside
the U.S. at 317-572-3986 or fax 317-572-4002. Jossey-Bass also publishes its books in a
variety of electronic formats. Some content that appears in print may not be available in
electronic books.

Unless otherwise noted, Bible quotations are from the *New Revised Standard Version Bible,*
copyright 1989, Division of Christian Education of the National Council of the Churches of
Christ in the United States of America. Used by permission. All rights reserved.

Excerpt from PRAYERS FROM THE HEART by RICHARD J. FOSTER. Copyright ©
1994 by Richard J. Foster. Reprinted by permission of HarperCollins Publishers Inc.

"Midwife of Our Lives" by Kathy Galloway from *The Pattern of Our Days: Liturgies and
Resources for Worship,* Kathy Galloway (ed). Copyright © 1996 Kathy Galloway. Published
by Wild Goose Publications, Glasglow G2 3DH Scotland.

Library of Congress Cataloging-in-Publication Data

Farrington, Debra K.
Learning to hear with the heart : meditations for discerning God's will / Debra K.
Farrington.— 1st ed.
p. cm.
Includes bibliographical references.
ISBN 0-7879-6716-5 (alk. paper)
1. Christian life—Meditations. 2. Discernment (Christian theology)—Meditations. 3.
God—Will—Meditations. I. Title.
BV4509.5 .F375 2003
242—dc21   2002152400

Printed in the United States of America
FIRST EDITION
HB Printing   10 9 8 7 6 5 4 3 2 1

Contents

Let me hear what God the LORD will speak,
for he will speak peace to his people, to his faithful,
to those who turn to him in their hearts.
—PSALM 85:8

Acknowledgments

I will sing to the Lord, for he has dealt with me richly," writes the Psalmist (Ps. 13:6, BCP translation). And one of the ways in which God has richly blessed me is with lots of people who have taught me to hear with my own heart by showing me how they do it. There isn't room to acknowledge and thank all of them for that here, but I am grateful for all of those in my life, now and in the past, who have encouraged me to dig deeper and listen more clearly for God's presence and guidance in my life.

For the invitation to write this book, I thank Sheryl Fullerton, my editor, colleague, and friend. Sheryl seems to know what I need to write before I do, which is evidence of her own hearing heart. I am grateful for her guidance, companionship, and patience, which nurture me personally and professionally. I thank the entire Jossey-Bass team as well. Their enthusiasm for my words and their professionalism and skill in making them better, packaging them beautifully, and telling the world about them are deeply appreciated.

My thanks go, as well, to Barbara Crafton, who writes some of the best meditations I have ever read. Barbara added me to her list of nearly daily e-mail meditations a year or so ago, and those wonderful missives have been my teachers and perpetual inspiration. How she comes up with the gems she sends out on a nearly daily basis, I'll never know, but I look forward to them and continue to learn from her.

My thanks also go to Nancy Fitzgerald, Val Gittings, and Phyllis Tickle. All three are women who hear with their hearts, and I'm grateful for their assistance in helping me listen to what this book needed to say and for improving my thinking and writing when needed. Finally, my thanks go to Linda Roghaar, my agent, for her unflagging support and encouragement.

D.K.F.

Introduction

Solomon had only been king a short while when he went to Gibeon to offer a sacrifice to God, as was the custom at that time. At Gibeon, God appeared to Solomon in a dream. "Ask for what I should give you," God commanded Solomon. Solomon's reply was a humble one. After recounting God's great favor to his father, King David, Solomon continued: "I am only a little child; I do not know how to go out or come in. And your servant is in the midst of the people whom you have chosen, a great people, so numerous they cannot be numbered or counted. Give your servant therefore an understanding mind to govern your people, able to discern between good and evil; for who can govern this your great people?" (1 Kings 3:7–9).

Various translations of the Bible convey Solomon's request as one of an understanding mind or heart, and sometimes as wisdom. But the literal translation of the Hebrew indicates that Solomon asked for a "hearing heart," one with which he could discern between good and evil. Using a hearing heart for discernment doesn't mean that he was asking for stronger emotions or feelings for judging wisely. The ancient Hebrews thought of the heart as the center not only of emotions but also of intellect, physical health, and spiritual well-being. The heart was where you met and knew God most deeply. So when Solomon asked that God help his heart—his intellect, body, and soul—listen for and hear God's guidance in order to discern well and clearly, he wanted God's will to inform every aspect of his life. You can ask for and receive this same gift as well.

This book of meditations is for those who want a companion on their discernment journey. If you are also reading my other book, *Hearing with the Heart: A Gentle Guide to Discerning God's Will for Your Life,* you will be getting lots of detailed information about the process of discernment. This book of meditations is different. I intend for them to help you explore—with your mind, body, and soul—some of the different ways in which you can open up your heart and hear. It uses evocative material—poetry, Scripture, stories—to help you do that.

Discernment—literally the "separating apart"—of God's desires for you from all the other ones in the world sounds to some people like a cerebral process and to others like a mystical one. It is both, neither, and more. Hearing with your heart requires that you become more aware and alert intellectually, emotionally, spiritually, and physically. The meditations in this book invite you to explore all of those avenues.

Discernment also requires that we have a relationship with God like the one Solomon had. Solomon had no qualms about talking freely with God. He wasn't afraid to ask for what he truly needed. He didn't try to disguise his strengths and weaknesses. And while he humbled himself by alluding to himself as only a child, his humility didn't prevent him from believing that God wanted to give him exactly what he needed to carry out God's desires for his life. Solomon knew himself as God's beloved and wasn't surprised that God would talk to him or offer him gifts.

The same is true for you and me. We are all God's beloved, and God cares deeply about what we think and feel and about the gifts we need to live out God's dream for the world. In fact, God speaks to us through the desires of our own hearts many times. God, the Creator, planted those desires in our hearts, the same hearts that, when open and listening, can discern and live out God's will. That isn't to say that every desire you feel comes from God, and I'll explore that in some of the meditations here, but your most deeply felt desires—the most persistent ones—are sometimes clues to what God would have you do and be. To ignore or distrust them deprives you of important information.

This book sees discernment as an everyday kind of activity rather than as something to be saved for crossroads or crisis moments. In fact, discerning God's will at those major moments in your life is easier if you're in the habit of practicing discernment regularly. God desires a just and peaceful world—one where every created being or thing has what it needs to live. So actions like deciding how to vote, what foods and resources to consume, and how to treat others and the earth are all opportunities to practice discerning God's desires.

Those practices involve teaching your mind, body, and soul to be more attentive to God's dreams and how they are communicated to you. Some ways of practicing are outlined in detail in my book *Hearing with the Heart,* but some brief pointers to areas to explore follow here. The first four are suggestions for practicing attentiveness in everyday discerning; the last two are particularly helpful when you are facing a big decision and need some extra tools.

Pray

"Pray without ceasing," writes Paul in 1 Thessalonians, and that's what you need to do to discern well. That doesn't mean you need to be in church or at the local monastery 24/7. Prayer isn't only formal words and worship; it's just conversation with God. There are lots of ways to pray, but prayer that's a two-way, rather than a one-way, conversation is what matters most for discernment. There's absolutely nothing wrong with telling God what you need, or praying for the needs of others, but coming to know God's desires involves listening and hearing with your heart as well.

One of the ways to do that is to practice being silent in prayer. On the radio news recently, I head a story about someone who created a device that simulates the experience of schizophrenia. The reporter played a taped segment of what the person using the device hears, and even a few seconds of it frightened me. Too many voices were talking, each on top of the other, with not a moment's break in the din. I got a sense of how painful the experience of schizophrenia must be and how difficult it is for reality to break through all of those chaotic voices.

Our own minds are usually not as cluttered or painful as the minds of those who suffer with schizophrenia, but most of us still find it difficult to turn off the voices that chatter about the day or whatever else is on our mind, and listen for the voice of God. Western culture discourages the practice of silence, often confusing it with loneliness. Most of us are practiced at receiving and processing a variety of messages through our different senses simultaneously. Doing one thing at a time, or doing nothing, is foreign and uncomfortable for many people. But without spending some time in silence—without befriending it—hearing the voice of God is difficult, if not impossible. If you're talking all the time, God won't be able to get a word in edgewise, and if God can't get a word in, you'll have no way of discerning what you're called to be or do.

If practicing silence is new for you, it might be helpful to practice it as you read the daily meditations in this book. Take five minutes before reading each day's meditation and just sit still in silence, even if it feels awkward at first. After practicing this for a week or so, you'll probably begin to discover a richness in the silence that you didn't know before.

Hearing with your heart involves not only silence in prayer but also openness to whatever you hear as well. It isn't always what you expect. So many formal prayers include requests that God do this or that, and there's nothing wrong with saying them. But discernment involves listening for God's desires, some of which may come as a surprise. We sit (or stand or walk) in expectant silence when we're practicing discernment, waiting and hoping to hear with our hearts. To listen for God's agenda, it's necessary to try to let go of your own agendas as you work with the material in this book. Or, if your own desires keep surfacing, pay attention to them and ask God to speak more clearly to you about what those desires might mean.

Only rarely will you get a sudden and dramatic response to praying this way. Occasionally God speaks clearly, as God did from a burning bush when talking to Moses. Most of the time, the process is subtler than that, so take time to notice how well you're listening. It's easy to think nothing's happening or that we're not hearing well when the communication is subtle. The practice of the Prayer of *Examen* is particularly useful for learning to notice what you've actually heard or done. The meditation on page 72 will guide you through that simple practice if it's new for you.

Pay Attention

Discernment is all about paying attention, but it's especially about becoming familiar with how God speaks to you through your gifts, your body, and the story of your life.

God gives gifts to all of us, ones that may provide clues to what God hopes we will do or be. Gifts are those skills or attributes that seem to come naturally to us, ones that we can exercise without even thinking much about them. Maybe you're good at math, or a good listener, or a natural leader. Your gifts can be just about anything.

Knowing what those gifts are, being aware of them and able to name and claim them, helps in discernment; those very gifts are often clues to what we are called to be or do. In the name of modesty or being humble, people sometimes fail to notice or recognize their gifts. Throughout this book, I'll invite you to pay attention to them and to the message they might carry for you.

Our bodies also provide clues to judging rightly, and, like our gifts, they are often ignored in the discernment process. Bodies have often been considered enemies or at least distractions throughout the history of Christian spirituality, but today many see them more as partners, particularly for the practice of discernment. Bodies "speak" to us and often tell us what's going on emotionally and spiritually before we're aware of that consciously.

The clues that our bodies provide aren't foolproof, but good and clear discernment is often accompanied by a relaxation of muscles, deep breathing (versus shallow breathing), a sense of released tension, and other feelings of well-being. Bodies can also warn us about moves in wrong directions. Have you ever made a decision and had a stomachache or headache for days afterward? Bodies give important clues to us when they respond to a decision with increased stress or pain in the body, shallow breathing, headache, and other unpleasant bodily sensations.

That doesn't mean that every illness or bodily pain is related to what's going on emotionally or spiritually. Germs exist in this world, and so do lots of diseases. But with a little practice, you'll be able to distinguish stress responses from illness. Most of us have a particular set of stress responses that our bodies use consistently to tell us we're stressed. And if you have a question about whether you're experiencing stress or some other difficulty, consult your doctor. Every body is different, and your stress responses may be different from mine. Get to know your body, and pay attention to the clues it provides. Considering your body as a partner in discernment will help you hear better with your heart.

Finally, I invite you to listen to your own life story once in a while. Think, for a minute, about how you told the story of your life five years ago, and then ten or twenty years ago, or before that. What were the main themes of your life's story line? They've probably changed over the years. That's largely because hindsight allows you to see the story differently as time passes. Something happens in the present that makes sense of something that happened in the past, and the story of your life shifts slightly. Take time to tell yourself or others the story of your life occasionally, and listen for the ways in which you have sensed God's guidance in the past—guidance that may be pointing you into the future.

Study

You may be surprised to find a suggestion that study is important to the practice of discernment. But don't forget that the Hebrews thought of the heart as the center of the intellect, as well as of the body, spirit, and emotions. A hearing heart needs nourishment for the mind if it is to hear well.

In *All I Really Need to Know I Learned in Kindergarten,* contemporary writer Robert Fulghum tells the story of his next-door neighbor, who, dressed for work, runs smack dab into a huge spider web. She runs screaming from the web and dashes inside, no doubt to wash every inch of her body and hair. Then Fulghum tells the story from the side of the spider—how she had created this wonderful web, one she's worked very hard to construct, and then this huge human being comes crashing into it, wrecking the whole thing.[1] There's always more than one way to see things, and that's why studying—seeing things through the eyes of others—helps you be a better discerner.

God works in more ways than you or I will ever see or understand, and the more of them we know about, the better our chances of seeing God's hand at work in our world and lives. Some of the meditations in this book invite you to think about your own image of God and how that affects your ability to discern and what you hear. There's always more than one way to understand and interpret what you hear or see. Someone else's understanding of God and how God has worked in his or her life may well open up new vistas for you. So read Scripture, but look, too, for other avenues of learning. God can work through anything, not just through Scripture. Read books of all sorts, watch television or attend the theatre, listen to music, look at art, attend lectures or classes. All of these, and more, are ways of studying and opening yourself up to God's hopes and desires.

Find Spiritual Companionship

St. Brigit of Kildare, one of the Celtic saints, said it best: "Anyone without a soul friend is like a body without a head."[2] Discernment by yourself, without consulting friends, family, a spiritual director, or some other part of your spiritual community, is incomplete and, potentially, inaccurate. It's way too easy to fool ourselves into believing that we know what God wills for us or to convince ourselves that God's dream for us matches our own, instead of matching our dream to God's. Consulting members of our spiritual community about what we're hearing in our hearts and seeking their confirmation or challenge is an important part of discerning well and clearly.

As an editor for a religious publisher, I routinely get manuscripts from authors who claim that their book was divinely inspired. That may be true, but I am always suspicious of anyone's sure and absolute knowledge that God told them to write something very specific. "Do not despise the words of prophets, but test everything; hold fast to what is good," says 1 Thessalonians 5:20–21. And one of the best ways to test what you're hearing is by consulting others whom you trust. Spiritual friends or guides can challenge you to dig a little deeper when needed, or they can affirm what you're hearing. Sometimes they can help you when what you hear confuses you or doesn't make a lot of sense. A good friend may also challenge you once in a while, when she thinks you may be listening to your own ego or to the call of the world around you instead of to God.

That isn't to say that your soul friends or spiritual guides will always be right. Test everything, as 1 Thessalonians advises. But if all of your trusted spiritual advisers suggest that you aren't hearing something clearly, that's a good reason for taking a little more time with your discernment or moving more slowly in making a final decision.

Balance Reason and Imagination

While we all use a combination of both reason and imagination to get through life, most people tend to rely on one more than the other. Some people are quick to get out paper and pencil and make a list of pros and cons, while others prefer to sit quietly and imagine what the consequences of taking a certain path might be. Because hearing with the heart involves mind, body, and soul, good discernment requires that you use both reason and imagination in listening for God's will.

St. Ignatius, the sixteenth-century saint whose classic *Spiritual Exercises* still informs the practice of discernment today, suggests that those in the midst of discernment use the following procedure. First, make a pro and con list, and then, using just the hard, cold facts, ask which path is more reasonable.

Then, using your imagination, explore three different scenarios. First, imagine that you are giving advice to someone else in the same position you're in. What advice would you give? Then, assume you are on your deathbed and look back at your life. Would you be pleased with the decision you are contemplating? Finally, Ignatius suggests you imagine yourself on judgment day, facing God. If that last image feels too harsh, just imagine yourself in conversation with God and leave out the part about judgment day. How do you think God would rate the path you're contemplating?

At the end of this process, says Ignatius, you should take your conclusions to God in prayer and try to sense if God confirms the decision you've come to. Confirmation may come in a sense of well-being, or of being one with God. But once you sense God's confirmation of your decision, it's wise to check that with a trusted friend or spiritual guide as well. Ignatius's exercises are usually done in conjunction with spiritual guidance. Even if you're doing this exercise privately, getting confirmation of what you've heard or felt from God is important.

So, as an example, if you were thinking of getting married, you might begin by making a pro and con list about married life with your intended partner. I've always been surprised by some of the things that end up on my pro and con list; often there are things on it that I wasn't conscious of before writing them down. Looking at that list, you would try to see what the reasonable decision should be.

Once you'd completed the list, you would try to imagine what advice you would give someone in your shoes, and then take your own advice as the best path for yourself. Then you would try to imagine how you'd feel, from your deathbed, about having chosen that path. There's no way to know for sure how you'd feel, of course, but use your imagination to try to construct what your life together might look like, and try to sense if that would be a pleasure to remember or a source of regret at the end of your life. Finally, imagine yourself telling God about the decision and why you'd make the one you had. Using all that you've learned from your list and your imaginings, see if a direction comes clear and bring that to God in prayer.

You'd be surprised how many things you learn by going through a process like this. If you can avoid censoring yourself and let your thoughts flow freely, you'll probably discover things about yourself and the issue under consideration that you didn't know about before.

Balance Patience and Action

Another set of characteristics to balance in the discernment process is patience and right action. Just as we have preferences about reason and imagination, we usually have a preference either for getting things decided and acted upon or for keeping the options open so that no doors are closed. The trick in discernment is figuring out when patience is called for and when it is time to act.

Patience is something of a neglected concept today. Though it is one of the classic Christian virtues, patience isn't even listed in contemporary dictionaries of theology or spirituality. In common usage, being patient implies that you're being a dishrag, putting up with all kinds of abuse without uttering a single complaint. Let me suggest a different way to think about patience in discernment. Patience is staying engaged with God, no matter how frustrating the discernment process gets. Impatience is making a decision even when you have no sense of being invited in one direction or another. It is dismissing God from the decision-making process. Patience is hanging in there, even when it means being angry or frustrated with God's silence or the indecisiveness you feel. Patience is continuing to ask for—or even demand—an answer and staying in the conversation until you get one.

Answers don't always come in complete sentences or paragraphs in a clear booming voice from heaven, however. Bells, whistles, and lights don't flash when you get the "right" answer in discernment. Most of the time, what you get are snippets of sentences, glimmers of the path ahead. You'll have a sense that one path seems like the right one. And that's what you'll need to act on. You just have to follow what your heart is telling you and see what happens. Not every discernment will result in the "perfect answer," but I don't think there are any totally wrong answers either. Even a misstep can become your teacher. One of the most miserable jobs I ever held was the result of a clear misstep on my part, and I could have done without the experience. But I learned a whole lot, and what I learned has helped me avoid similar mistakes since that time. No decision—unless it's life threatening—is final. You can always make a different decision and try another path.

How to Use This Book

Whether you are reading this book because you have a pressing concern or because you just want to know more about discernment, it is helpful to begin by being aware of one question or issue you'd like to explore while you're reading the meditations that follow. That can be a decision that you're facing right now, or if there's nothing major to discern, use something that's part of your everyday life, such as how to use your financial resources, what kind of volunteer work you might be called to, or how to interact with friends or family members who are close to you. It doesn't matter which issue you pick, but it will be helpful to focus the conversation with God on a specific question.

Thirty days of meditations follow, arranged into four weeks, with a few days at the end to reflect on your time with God. I've provided one meditation for each day, along with a focus question to help you apply the meditation to whatever you're working on. A closing prayer is also included for each day. If you have a little bit of time to give to reading and discerning each day, you might want to begin by spending five minutes in silence and quieting your mind. Then read the meditation, and either silently consider the focus question or journal about it if you find that helpful. Close your time with the prayer when you're ready.

On the last day of each of the four weeks, I've included a more extensive exercise based on Martin Luther's way of reading Scripture. His was a way of practicing what is called *lectio divina,* or sacred reading. Instructions are provided each week, but the basic practice is to read the passage given several times, using a different focus question to guide your reading each time. Give yourself at least half an hour to do this exercise.

Debra K. Farrington
Harrisburg, Pennsylvania
February 2003

Of Beginnings and Foundations

DAY 1

Ask the Right Question

> The same day some Sadducees came to him, saying there is no resurrection; and they asked him a question. . . .
>
> —MATTHEW 22:23

*P*art of the fun of reading murder mysteries is trying to solve the crime before the author does it for you. I can't claim any great skill in this area. Maybe I'm just a slow learner, or too trusting. More charitably, I like to think that mystery writers are particularly good at throwing me a curve. Time after time my experience is the same as that of many of the fictional sleuths: I ask the wrong question, so I get the wrong answer.

Discernment isn't much different from reading mysteries in that way. The Sadducees found that out for themselves. Trying to figure out who Jesus was—trying to trip him up, they asked him a question: "Teacher, Moses said, 'If a man dies childless, his brother shall marry the widow, and raise up children for his brother.' Now there were seven brothers among us; the first married, and died childless, leaving the widow to his brother. The second did the same, so also the third, down to the seventh. Last of all, the woman herself died. In the resurrection, then, whose wife of the seven will she be?" (Matthew 22:24–28). Jesus' answer was not the one they expected. No one marries in the resurrection, he said, so the question was irrelevant. Ask the wrong question, you get the wrong answer.

So much of discernment hinges on asking the right question, and it's so easy to ask the wrong one. That's why Ignatius of Loyola, the sixteenth-century saint whose *Spiritual Exercises* was mentioned earlier, recommends that we spend some time clarifying the question before we start discerning the answer. Think of it like this. I've had minor back problems for years, and when I go to the chiropractor with one complaint, I often discover that the source of the problem actually lies somewhere other than where I thought it was. The surface pain is just masking some deeper problem. That's what happens in discernment sometimes. You're trying to figure out if you should take this path or that one, when the actual question might be whether you should move at all. What's the motivation for moving? Are you running toward something or just away from something? Ignore those questions, and persist in trying to discern which path to take, and you probably won't feel a clear sense of call in any direction. Ask the wrong question . . . well, you know what happens.

Answers are almost always more satisfying than questions. I'm always tempted to jump to the end of my murder mysteries and find the solution to the crime without having to read the whole book. But staying with the questions is part of the process. "Try to love the questions themselves," says German poet and writer Rainer Maria Rilke.[1]

We want answers quickly in today's world. We've gotten used to having instant answers from others via phone, fax, or e-mail, and it's easy to want that from God as well. But good discernment depends on asking good questions, and that means we need to sit with them for a while and make sure they're the right ones to ask. Love the questions, as Rilke recommends. The answers will come in due time.

What question do you bring to this month of discernment time?

O heavenly Father, the author and fountain of all truth, the bottomless sea of all understanding, send, we beseech thee, thy Holy Spirit into our hearts, and lighten our understandings with the beams of thy heavenly grace.
—NICHOLAS RIDLEY

DAY 2

Who Do You Say I Am?

Your word is a lamp to my feet and a light to my path.
—PSALM 119:105

What's your image of God? If you were to look at all of the biblical names and metaphors for God, which ones would speak most truthfully to you? There are lots of reasons to believe in a wrathful God—the one who flooded the earth and drowned everything except Noah and two of each animal, the one who destroyed Sodom and Gomorrah and turned Lot's wife into a pillar of salt in the process, the one who, per Job's friends' image of God, punished Job for wrongdoings he couldn't even remember. This is the God Jonathan Edwards, an eighteenth-century clergyman and preacher, pictured as holding us over the pit of hell, just as an unfeeling child might hold a spider over a flame.

There are also a lot less fearsome images of God in the Bible. God freed the Israelites from slavery. God is a mustard seed that grows into a huge shrub that provides a place for birds to nest. God is the shepherd who rejoices to find one lost sheep. God welcomes the prodigal back home.

All of these images and more are found in the biblical texts, and they all have something to say to us. But the overall image of God that you take away from that reading will have everything to do with what you discern as God's desires for you. Think about the parable of the Good Samaritan (Luke 10:30–36) in that light.

A man lay naked, beaten, and near death by the side of the road. The first two travelers to pass by him—a Judean priest and a Levite—were officials of the Temple. To touch someone who was dead would make them unclean and unfit for their duties. Priests and Levites weren't even allowed to attend a funeral unless it was for a close relative of theirs. The God they knew demanded purity from them and bound them with rules and regulations focused on serving God alone rather than their neighbors.

The Samaritan came next. The Judeans and the Samaritans hated each other, though they were both Jewish. The Samaritans didn't observe the same laws of purity and cleanliness that the Judeans found important. And the Samaritan, apparently, was not a priest. Some scholars surmise that he was a trader, since he seemed to travel with a good bit of cash. We don't know much about the Samaritan's theology, but Jesus used him as an example of someone who considered everyone his neighbor and worthy of loving care.

Each of the three men acted on his own understanding of God's desires for him. The Levite and the priest believed that God desired their ritual cleanliness and so they avoided the dying man by the roadside. The Samaritan seemed to hold a different image of what God required, and so he took the man to an inn and cared for him. How they imaged God influenced what they discerned of God's desires and how they acted on those.

"Who do you say I am?" Jesus asked Peter in the gospels. And that is the question for us as well. Who do you say God is? Once you have answered that question you'll probably find it easier to discern what God's desires are for you.

What images of God do you find most compelling? Why?

Grant us the knowledge that we need
*   To solve the questions of the mind;*
Light thou our candles while we read,
*   To keep our hearts from going blind;*
Enlarge our vision to behold
The wonders Thou hast wrought of old;
Reveal Thyself in every law,
And gild the towers of truth with holy awe.
        —HENRY VAN DYKE

DAY 3

Follow Your Own Path

You show me the path of life. In your presence there is fullness of joy; in your right hand are pleasures forevermore.

—Psalm 16:11

In his book *The Song of the Bird* Catholic priest and story-teller Anthony De Mello tells a wonderful story. One day a man saw a fox with no legs and he wondered how the fox survived. A moment later a tiger with game in his mouth came along and dropped it off for the fox to eat. Day after day, this continued, and the man was astonished at how God provided for the fox through the tiger. "'I too shall just rest in a corner with full trust in the Lord and he will provide me with all I need,'" the man said.[1] The man did just that, but no one brought him food and he nearly died. Finally he heard a voice: "'O you who are in the path of error, open your eyes to the truth! Follow the example of the tiger and stop imitating the disabled fox.'"[2]

Life—and discernment—would be so much easier if we could just imitate what others do, if we all had the same path and didn't have to try to find the way ourselves. But life doesn't come with a map and instruction book. Finding your own path is part of the difficulty—and also part of the fun. There are so many paths to choose from, but only some of them will be the ones God calls you to walk, as a story from the Desert Fathers shows:

> One of the monks asked the great teacher Abba Nistero: "What should I do for the best in life?" And the abba answered: "All works are not equal. The Scripture says that Abraham was hospitable, and God was with him; it says that Elias loved quiet, and God was with him; it says that David was humble, and God was with him. So, whatever path you find your soul longs after in the quest for God, do that, and always watch over your heart's integrity."[3]

Each of us has a different path to walk. We don't know much about the fox's path in the story above, but feeding the fox was part of the tiger's path. The man's mistake was that he thought his path was the same as the fox's. His was a perfectly natural error, one we all make at some time or another. We look at a system or strategy that's working for someone else and think it will solve our problem or improve our life, too. Or a kindly friend offers advice about what worked for her, sure that it will work just as well for us. Sometimes that's true, and sometimes it isn't. The man missed seeing that his path was more like the tiger's than the fox's. And even if his path were more like the tiger's, it wasn't identical to the tiger's path. After all, that particular tiger took care of his particular fox. If the man's path was to care for someone, he needed to find his own "fox."

If the same systems worked for everyone there would be no need for discernment—we could just follow the rules and all would be well. I don't know about you, but to me that sounds pretty dull. It can be frustrating to try to discern my path, but I'd rather do that than just have an instruction card handed to me at birth. Finding my own fox may be a nuisance some days, but for the most part, it's a grand adventure.

When have you started walking down someone else's path instead of your own? What was the result of that experience?

O thou full of compassion,
I commit and commend myself unto thee,
in whom I am,
and live,
and know.
Be thou the goal of my pilgrimage,
and my rest along the way.
　　　—St. Augustine

DAY 4

Join God's Club

Do not withhold; bring my sons from far away and my daughters from the end of the earth—everyone who is called by my name, whom I created for my glory, whom I formed and made.

—ISAIAH 43:6–7

Maybe you've seen Woody Allen's classic movie *Annie Hall*. In it there's a scene where the two main characters, Annie and Alvy, have their first real conversation as they circle around each other, trying to discover if there might be the possibility of a romantic relationship between them. Ostensibly they're talking about modern art, but what they're actually trying to do is impress and evaluate the other. As they talk, what they're really thinking appears on the screen as subtitles for us to read. The subtitles show us that they're really worried about how stupid they think they sound, or that the other person might not like them. Their hearts are so wrapped up in worry that they can't actually hear very much of what's happening. They weren't being very good at discerning anything at that particular moment.

I've had some conversations with God that felt just like Annie and Alvy's. Have you ever felt that God couldn't possibly love you as you are, that if God only knew how awful you really were at the core, God wouldn't be calling you Beloved? Woody Allen quotes a line from Groucho Marx later in *Annie Hall:* "I wouldn't want to belong to a club that would have me for a member." And we all nod knowingly when he says it. Allen fears that only a club full of losers would want him for a member. And I don't know about you, but I have days when I wonder if God feels that way about me.

The reality of the unconditional love of God conflicts with so many other messages insisting that whatever you want must be earned, and you only get what you deserve. God becomes the cosmic schoolteacher, doling out the appropriate performance-based grades, not the lover of our souls. But discernment—hearing with the heart—becomes very difficult if we see God this way. Who wants to spend time discerning the desires of a God who sees us as losers? And if God sees us as losers, why would God bother to take the time to communicate with us at all?

But we're not losers. We're the beloved sons and daughters of a loving God—one who has many promises, hopes, and dreams to share with us. "I have called you by name, you are mine," God says in Isaiah 43:1. If you feel like you're an unlikely candidate for being called by God, look at some of the unlikely characters God called in the biblical stories. Moses wasn't a leading politician, the likely choice for rescuing the slaves from Egypt. Poor Jonah never did quite get with the program and understand God's call to him completely, at least not in the story as told in the

Bible. He just kept complaining the whole way through. No matter. God keeps calling us—all of us—even if we're not the obvious choice for the job.

There's no need to talk with God as Alvy talked with Annie in the movie, no need to worry that God is thinking something awful about us as we talk. God didn't say, "I have called most of you by name. Those of you that I specifically named are mine." There is not one of us who is unworthy of receiving a call from God. Not one of us is a loser in God's book. God is always happy to be a member of a club that would have us for a member as well, to paraphrase the opposite of what Groucho Marx once said.

What factors in your own life have affected your sense of worthiness or unworthiness to receive a call from God?

Lord, grant us eyes to see
Within the seed a tree,
Within the glowing egg a bird,
Within the shroud a butterfly:
Till taught by such, we see
Beyond all creatures thee,
And hearken for thy tender word
And hear it, "Fear not: it is I."
—CHRISTINA ROSSETTI

DAY 5

Is Your Prayer Too Small?

When you are praying, do not heap up empty phrases as the Gentiles do; for they think that they will be heard because of their many words.

—MATTHEW 6:7

She came up to me after one of my presentations with a discouraged look on her face. "I bought your book," she said, "and I started reading it, but I did terribly on the first exercise." The exercise she referred to asked readers to make a list of the things that nurtured their spirits. I didn't know that it was possible to do poorly on the task, so I asked her why she thought that was so. "Most of the things I listed had to do with being out in nature instead of worship and regular prayer times," she responded. It sounded to me like she'd done just fine with her list.

Years ago a book called *Your God Is Too Small* was published. It argued that we have too narrow an image of God, one that reduces God to less than what God is. I sometimes think I'd like to write a book called *Your Prayer Is Too Small*—for all of us who sometimes think that God only hears us when we worship within a community or say the formal prayers of our faith traditions. That's why I often ask groups to make a list of the things that nurture their spirit.[1] Their lists usually include a wonderful variety of things—walks in the woods, digging in the garden, playing with the dog, making love, singing in the choir, helping children with their homework, and hundreds of other ways in which people experience the presence of God. All of these become ways of praying once we recognize that God is present in those times, places, and activities, especially when we begin to understand that prayer is no more—and no less—than conversation with God. Conversations don't need to be carefully scripted; they just need at least two participants who take turns listening and speaking.

Don't misunderstand me; I love church services and the formal prayers in my prayer book. But when I am praying in hopes of discerning God's call to me, I find the simpler, less scripted prayer times to be the most helpful. It's the walking-around-the-lake prayer, the pulling-weeds-in-the-garden prayer, or the staring-off-into-space variety of prayer that leaves me most open to God's voice. Maybe these work best because the mind wanders more freely than it does during more formal prayers. Perhaps when we're daydreaming, walking, gardening, and doing other activities, God is more like the best friend who comes up quietly and makes a fascinating comment or observation. Or maybe we're just more receptive when we're not expecting God to talk to us at a given moment. I don't know how prayer communication with God works any more than you do. All I know is that God has many ways of speaking to us and that God isn't bound by any four walls. So if finding God in the garden or woods helps your heart to hear more deeply, by all means, dig in the dirt and wander in the woods as often as you can.

What are the things that nurture your spirit? How can those places or activities be prayer for you?

Hear my prayer, O God; give ear to the words of my mouth.
—PSALM 54:2

DAY 6

Read the Bible Again

So Philip ran up to it and heard him reading the prophet Isaiah. He asked, "Do you understand what you are reading?"
—ACTS 8:30

I'm really fortunate that I wasn't a student in her class. A friend of mine, a clergyperson, gives all the teenagers in her confirmation classes a quiz. Their experience is usually the same as mine was: abysmal failure.

You try some of these questions: Were Joseph and Mary married when Jesus was born? What did the innkeeper say to Joseph when Joseph came looking for a place to rest? Was Jesus delivered in a stable or a manger? What is a "heavenly host"? The answers seem simple enough, but I'll bet some of you got them wrong just as I did. See Luke 2:5 and you'll discover that Joseph and Mary were only engaged when Jesus was born. And try as you might, you won't find an innkeeper in the nativity stories. Try to find out where Jesus was born and you won't find that either. And did you know that a heavenly host is an angel army? I thought I knew a little something about Scripture, but like most of us, I knew less than I thought. I wonder how often we base our discernment of God's will on biblical stories or instructions that we don't actually know very well. God's instructions get bandied about in public discourse, sometimes with little basis in Scripture. My clergy friend surprises the kids in her confirmation class by telling them that Jesus never told anyone to avoid sex before marriage—that this isn't in the Bible at all. (She tells them it's a good idea anyway, but that's a different point.) Public policy and decisions about sexuality and proper behavior of all sorts get made on the basis of what we *think* is in Scripture—or on small snippets of biblical text taken out of context. But what's really inside the pages of that book we consider holy and authoritative for our lives?

In 1995 I read a story in Phyllis Tickle's book *Rediscovering the Sacred: Spirituality in America* that completely changed my perspective on suffering. In her book, Tickle retold the story in Numbers where Moses' rebellious crowd is again complaining about God as they wander in the desert, and their camp is suddenly infested with snakes. People were dying, and they begged Moses to ask God for help, which he did. God instructed Moses to create a bronze snake, which he put on a cross pole and carried around the camp. All who looked up at the snake on the pole lived. They weren't spared snakebites but they didn't die from them. I'm still astonished that I never heard or read that biblical story—a powerful one about suffering and what God can do for us in the midst of it. What I discern of God's presence in my own suffering will forever be colored by the story of those Israelites in the desert.

I have often used biblical stories to help me discern what I think God's desires might be for me. I've been comforted when my experiences seem to line up in significant ways with those of Moses or other biblical figures. But I think I just might go back and check out a few texts a bit more carefully in the future, especially the ones about Jesus' birth. I'm no longer quite so sure that I know the stories as they actually appear in the Bible, and I think I'd like to know what they have to say.

What biblical stories have influenced the ways in which you think God guides you?

Blessed God, by whose providence all Holy Scriptures were written and preserved for our instruction: give us grace to study them each day with patience and love; strengthen our souls with the fullness of their divine teaching; keep us from all pride and irreverence; guide us in the deep things of your heavenly wisdom; and, of your great mercy, lead us by your Word into everlasting life.
—BROOKE FOSS WESCOTT

Keep an Open and Hearing Heart

> Where were you when I laid the foundation of the earth?
> Tell me, if you have understanding.
> —GOD TO JOB, JOB 38:4

There was once a church bell, contemporary story-teller and author Edward Hays tells us, that was very proud of the work it did.[1] The bell thought of its work as holy. When it was time to pray, the bell rang. When someone in the town did something wrong, the bell preached a sermon. When someone missed an appointment, or did something rude, the bell scolded. It was hard work, but the bell did it well.

One day a wandering bell came into town and rested on the steps of the church. Seeing the opportunity for a brief vacation, the church bell asked the wandering bell to take its place for a few days, and the wandering bell was happy to oblige. The wandering bell did as the church bell had instructed. It rang out the times for prayer, and it preached the occasional sermon, but the tones of this new bell were different—so beautiful that the people of the town responded by praying and listening attentively. Even the animals and birds listened to the new bell.

Upon its return the church bell was so furious about how beloved the substitute bell had become that it demanded that the wandering bell leave immediately. The wandering bell responded to the church bell's anger with its usual gentle voice. Surprised, the church bell asked how the visiting bell could respond so graciously to anger. The visiting bell responded simply that it had been purified many times by the refiner's fire over the years and that all of its tones were now beautiful. The church bell, on the other hand, listened only to its own sense of duty, of what was proper and fitting, and imposed that on everyone around it.

More days than I would like to admit, I am like the church bell instead of the visitor. It is easier to impose my sense of what is correct on others instead of listening with an open and gentle heart. And I have found that this tendency to impose my thinking on others is one of the most difficult barriers to learning to live a discerning life. After all, if I know the right answer—not only for myself but for everyone else as well, what need do I have for discernment?

But good discernment requires that we grow more comfortable with not knowing, with being open to all sorts of possibilities. We have to accept that we don't know what God has in mind for us or for anyone else, that we weren't there when God laid the foundation of the earth, and that our knowledge is limited. It goes against much of what we've learned throughout our lives, and it goes especially against the natural desire or need to control what is happening around us. The truly wise men and women may well be the ones who can say, "I don't know" and maintain an open and hearing heart, rather than spending their days ringing out dutifully but dully.

Which bell are you more like? Why?

Lord, give us a heart to turn all knowledge to thy glory and not to our own. Keep us from being deluded with the lights of vain philosophies. Keep us from the pride of human reason. Let us not think our own thoughts; but in all things acting under the guidance of the Holy Spirit, may we find thee everywhere, and live in all simplicity, humility and singleness of heart unto the Lord.

—Henry Kirke White

Lectio: Resting in the Word

Begin this exercise by sitting quietly for a few moments, with your eyes open or closed—whichever works best to help you center your thoughts on where you are, rather than on the events of the day. Breathe deeply, and try to let the muscles of your body relax. When you are ready, open with this simple prayer:

> May the words of my mouth, and the meditations of my (our) heart(s) be acceptable to you, O God, my rock and my redeemer. Amen.

1. Read this poem—a restatement of Psalm 23 by seventeenth-century poet George Herbert—through slowly, and simply listen to what it is saying. What is the overall message of this passage? Allow yourself to just absorb the passage in silence for a couple of minutes.

The Twenty-Third Psalm
The God of love my shepherd is,
    And he that doth me feed:
While he is mine, and I am his,
    What can I want or need?
He leads me to the tender grass,
    Where I both feed and rest;
Then to the streams that gently pass:
    In both I have the best.
Or if I stray he doth convert
    And bring my mind in frame:

And all this not for my desert,
    But for his holy name.
Yea, in death's shady black abode
    Well may I walk, not fear:
For thou art with me; and thy rod
    To guide, thy staff to bear.
Nay, thou dost make me sit and dine,
    Ev'n in my enemies' sight:
My head with oil, my cup with wine
    Runs over day and night.
Surely thy sweet and wondrous love
    Shall measure all my days;
And as it never shall remove,
    So neither shall my praise.

2. Read the passage a second time. As you do, listen for a word or phrase that seems to be an instruction for you. Is there something that jumps out at you from the text that feels like God's instruction or guidance for your life? Make a note of that word or phrase, if you wish, and quietly contemplate that instruction for a few minutes before moving on.

3. Read the passage a third time. When you hear the passage you focused on in the second reading, allow yourself to experience a sense of gratitude for God's guidance in the word or words that stood out to you. Rest in that sense of thankfulness for a few minutes.

4. Read the passage for the fourth time. Do you hear a word or phrase that calls you to confession? Notice what you are feeling at this time, and respond to God as appropriate.

5. Read the passage a final time, and listen for an overall sense of guidance in the text. Find an image in your mind or in the words themselves that allows you to rest in God's guidance, even if you are not sure what God is asking of you.

If you are doing this exercise by yourself, you may wish to take a few minutes at the end of it and make some notes about your experiences and feelings while doing this. If you are doing this exercise with others, the group may find it helpful to allow some time for those who wish to share their thoughts and feelings.

Hearing All Ways

DAY 8

Pay Attention, Listen, and Learn

Pay attention, come to me; listen and your soul will live.
—Isaiah 55:3 (Jerusalem Bible)

"Looking back on it now, I can see there were signs," writes the middle-aged writer and narrator of Diane Schoemperlen's novel, *Our Lady of the Lost and Found*.[1] Faced with a weeklong visit from the Virgin Mary, the narrator realized that had she been paying attention, she would have known that something was up long before Mary appeared. A squirrel visited her window box three days in a row, staying for exactly one half hour each time. A list of malfunctioning appliances suddenly started to work perfectly. The local library had all the books she wanted. The bakery had one last loaf of her favorite cheese bread, and everything she needed from the drugstore was on sale. There were many more signs, but our narrator chalked it up to luck. Luck is easier to explain than signs in our scientific age.

I wonder if Moses' story was a bit like Schoemperlen's narrator's. Maybe he ignored a whole bunch of signs, too, or chalked up his good life to luck, and God finally got his attention with a burning bush. Think about it. Moses grew

29

up in Pharaoh's court, no doubt aware that he was a Hebrew child. Perhaps it was the stress of watching his own people being mistreated, while he lived in luxury, that made him finally snap and kill the overseer. To save his own life, he fled to Midian, where he married and lived what was probably a comfortable life, away from the stresses of Egypt and the plight of his people—out of sight and out of mind. But not out of the sight or mind of God.

I wonder if God sent signs to Moses long before the bush that appeared to be burning. Did Moses ignore travelers who told stories of the torture of the Hebrews in Egypt? Did he dream of those he'd left behind and then dismiss the dream in the morning? What did he tell his wife and her family about his life before he joined them, and how did he feel when he told them of his previous life? If Moses was anything like me, I bet he ignored all sorts of signs. Signs that something was coming. Maybe he was like Schoemperlen's narrator, who, upon hearing a faint sighing sound from behind the fig tree, dismissed it as her imagination, locked the door, turned out the lights, and went to bed. She got a visit from the Virgin Mary the next day, and Mary stayed for the week. Moses got a burning bush.

I've had a few surprises in my own life as well. On occasion, I'd done an excellent job of ignoring the signs, coincidences, dreams, and comments from others—for good long periods of time. God hasn't resorted to putting a burning bush in my path to communicate with me, but I've been inattentive enough to have earned one a few times. It's as if, metaphorically, I sometimes cover my ears and utter loud nonsense sounds, as children do so that they won't hear what their parent or teacher is saying. "Pay attention," God keeps saying to me, trying to get through the noise I'm making. "Pay attention, listen, and your soul will live."

I don't think I ignore God—and the signs—consciously or on purpose any more than Moses or Schoemperlen's narrator did. Sometimes I'm just toddling along in life, and discernment—reading the signs God sends me—just seems like too much work. And God probably doesn't need me to read the signs 24/7. But when God does have something important to say to me, and I ignore it long enough, I usually get some really blatant sign at some point, something hard to ignore. The upside is that God seems to be infinitely patient and keeps signaling me. I may be slow, or even lazy, some days, but God always gets through eventually.

If you look back, using that perfect 20/20 hindsight, what signs did you miss at the time and only notice later?

Although I have often abandoned you, O Lord, you have never abandoned me. Your hand of love is always outstretched towards me, even when I stubbornly look the other way. And your gentle voice constantly calls me, even when I obstinately refuse to listen.
—Teresa of Avila

Hearing the Heart's Desire

Then the angel of God said to me in the dream, "Jacob,"
and I said, "Here I am!"
—GENESIS 31:11

Jim Morris, the main character in the recent movie *The Rookie,* had pretty much forgotten his dream. An avid baseball player as a child, he was now a teacher who coached the high school's losing baseball team on the side. His students liked him but didn't consider him to be anything special—not until they saw him throw a ninety-five-mile-per-hour fastball in practice one day. His team, the Owls, lost almost every one of their games, so one day Jim confronted them and challenged them to stop giving up on themselves and start dreaming bigger. The Owls thought he should take his own advice, so they made a deal with him: if they won the season he had to go try out for a professional baseball team. They saw his gift and wanted him to pursue it.

It's so easy to tell others to go after their dreams, somthing you know God calls them to be or do. Seeing someone else's deepest desire is often easier than seeing—and acting on—our own. Somehow our heart closes down when we desire something that seems fanciful, impractical, or unobtainable. The voice of reason takes over and closes down our discerning heart.

Jim Morris let the voice of reason take over for a long time, and he got a lot of support for doing that from most of his family and friends. Jim had been injured a few times in the past while playing professional baseball and now had a family to care for. His wife was happy and relieved when he had given up baseball. His father, ever the responsible man, told Jim that it was okay to dream about what you *wanted* to do until it was time to do what you *had* to do. So Jim walked away from his dream and did what he had to do, and he did it with grace.

But Jim's students discovered his real gift when they watched his pitching. They saw the desire in his heart and knew that he had to pursue it. "It's funny that you can't see it," they told him, "but we can."

You can guess the outcome. The Owls won their baseball season. Each one congratulated Jim by coming by, slapping his hand, and saying, "It's your turn." So Jim had to go try out for a minor league team. He made the team and then was moved up to a major league team, where he played for two years. His family struggled with finances along the way, and they sacrificed while he went out on the road to pursue his dream. But they were so proud of him, and every single one of them—along with most of the town—supported him in pursuing what he was meant to do.

I wonder how often we put off paying attention to what our hearts desire because it seems impossible or impractical. "With God all things are possible" makes a great slogan, but it's hard to actually believe it and trust in it. Still, what if God's invitations to us come wrapped up in the guise of our heart's deepest desires? What if the desire itself was planted in our hearts just so we would take notice and do something about it? What if God keeps fueling that desire until we accept the gift in it, just as Jim Morris did? Maybe God is a lot like Jim Morris's students and keeps saying to us, "It's funny that you can't see your gift—the one your heart desires to use—but I can. It's your turn."

What dreams do you have that seem impractical, improbable, or unreasonable? What prevents you from pursuing your heart's desire?

Almighty God, in whom we live and move and have our being, who hast made us for thyself, so that our hearts are restless till they rest in thee: Grant us purity of heart and strength of purpose, that no selfish passion may hinder us from knowing thy will, no weakness from doing it; but that in thy light we may see light clearly, and in thy service find perfect freedom; through Jesus Christ our Lord.
—St. Augustine

DAY 10

Name Your Gifts

Now there are varieties of gifts, but the same Spirit. . . .
—1 Corinthians 12:4

It is so easy to see God's gifts in others. The next door neighbor who has a green thumb with the lawn and garden. The person in the office who sees the good in everyone. That tireless person in the parish who always seems to have time for one more volunteer project. The person who can write effortlessly. Or the presenter who holds audiences captivated. If you're anything like me, it is easier to identify and name other people's gifts than it is to list your own.

Mark, a character on one of my favorite television shows, didn't think he had any gifts. He was overweight, not exactly the image of the male romantic lead in those Hollywood movies, and he assumed that his weight was the only thing girls, and others, cared about. It took him many episodes to realize—and admit to himself—that he was attracted to one of his close friends, Diane, and then it took a whole lot more for him to realize that who he was and his gifts were attractive to Diane.

Mark was funny, smart, very observant, and kind. He gave his friends a lot of slack, accepted their faults, and

35

loved them anyway. But he discounted all of these gifts, or maybe he didn't even notice that he had them. He was content to live quietly in the shadows of his more extroverted and flamboyant friends. More often than not, he poked fun at his weight and made jokes at his own expense rather than engage in any intimate conversation. When Diane asked him why he made fun of himself so often he told her it was just so easy. And Mark was right. Discounting your gifts is much easier and safer than finding the courage to name them, claim them, and grow into them.

Naming them, though, is really the hard part. If I asked you to name your gifts right now, I suspect you'd be embarrassed. I was, when someone asked me to do that a couple years ago. We have this idea that if we're even remotely aware of our gifts we're conceited or arrogant. We're supposed to take note of other people's gifts and compliment them rather than focus on our own. But trying to discern what God calls you to do or be without looking at and naming your gifts is like trying to solve a mystery without clues. Your chances of success in discerning what you should be doing are about as good as your chances of guessing the villain from a murder mystery's list of characters before reading a single page of the book. God gave you those gifts, in part, so that you have what you need to be what God calls you to be. So read the clues.

Think about recognizing and naming your gifts from a different angle for a moment. Someone gives you a great gift on your birthday, something really nice. You know the correct response; no doubt, someone taught it to you when you were young. You say, "Thank you," and you wear the gift proudly, or you display it in a prominent place. You don't put it back in the box and bury it under a pile of shoes in the back of the closet. Well, the same is true of the gifts God gave you. "No one after lighting a lamp puts it under the bushel basket, but on the lampstand, and it gives light to all in the house," says Jesus in Matthew 5:15. Name your gifts, claim them, and let your light shine. It's a way of saying "Thank you" to God. And you wouldn't want to be rude to God, would you?

What are at least three of the gifts God gave you?

May the Lord be blessed for ever for the great gifts
that he has continually heaped upon me,
and may all that he has created be praised. Amen.
—TERESA OF AVILA

Listen to Your Body

Therefore my heart is glad, and my soul rejoices; my
body also rests secure.
—Psalm 16:9

I t usually starts out benignly. When something is wrong
with the way I'm living, or the decisions I'm making, my
body responds first with shallow—rather than full and
deep—breathing. Unfortunately, that's usually too subtle a
sign for me to notice, and inevitably my body needs to go
to a stage two alert. Stage two involves tightened stomach
muscles and a lack of appetite, which, if it goes on for too
many days, results in low energy. I'm better at noticing that
my body is trying to tell me something when this happens.
Perhaps, more accurately, I should confess that I usually
notice that something is up at this stage, but sometimes I
forge on anyway and ignore my body.

Bodies, however, don't particularly like being dismissed so lightly. Stage three comes next: back and neck
pain. You see, my body has a sense of humor. It seems to be
saying to me, "You're being a pain in the neck!" Sometimes
I pay attention. Sometimes I don't. When I don't, my
body's sense of humor disappears, and I suffer from insom-
nia. Two or three nights of very little sleep finally gets my
attention, and I've never been brave enough to push my

poor body beyond that point. At stage four, I usually back down the number of hours I'm spending at work, write the book the way it wants to be written instead of the way I'd planned, or whatever else I need to do to bring my life back into balance with God's desires for me.

"God wants us to have joy in our souls and health in our bodies," Hildegard of Bingen once told a novice who was being too harsh on herself and others.[1] Hildegard, a wise woman from the eleventh century, was a prophet, preacher, teacher, and diplomat, as well as a noted healer who paid a lot of attention to bodies and souls. She believed that the soul was the living breath of God breathed into the body and that the two worked as one. When they acted in accord with each other, all was well. When they didn't—when the body ignored God's will—depression resulted. Hildegard obviously wrote from her eleventh-century perspective, and modern science would quibble with some of what she wrote. Still, I find her basic idea— that the soul and the body respond to one another and function best when they work in concert—to be helpful. My body is expert at telling me when my soul is suffering— that is, when I choose to pay attention.

Now, that's not to say that all illness is caused by the heart and soul being out of sync somehow. Someone's appendix doesn't burst because he or she has failed to listen to or follow God's will. Hildegard, our expert healer, was sick often in her life, despite her holiness and deep connection to God. But many of us experience bodily discomforts when we're not listening to God, when our desires are not in sync with how we are called to live. A colleague of mine finally quit her job because she listened to her body's wisdom. She did her work efficiently and effectively, but she didn't really love the job. She was angry too often, and she went home with a headache every night. Hildegard would have approved of her leaving the job and finding something she loved to do instead. Her new work put her body and soul back into sync.

We live in a culture that too often ignores the body's wisdom. Being tough, able to work long hours, working despite illness, sleeping too little, and eating poorly are all condoned by a culture obsessed with productivity and instant gratification. Sometimes it seems as if there's very little time to just breathe and be, to stop and notice what we're feeling, what the body is trying to say to us. But I'm working to be a little bit more like Hildegard and a little less like a trader on Wall Street. I've mastered the art of paying attention to my body at stages three and four, and now I'm working on getting better at listening at stage two. In the long run, the goal is to pay attention at the beginning stage, when my breathing starts getting shallow. It seems to me that if God has bothered to blow living breath into me, the least I can do is pay attention to it.

How does your body communicate with you, both when it is at peace and when it is not?

Breathe on me, Breath of God,
fill me with life anew,
that I may love what thou dost love,
and do what thou wouldst do.

Breathe on me, Breath of God,
until my heart is pure,
until with thee I will one will,
to do or to endure.

Breathe on me, Breath of God,
till I am wholly thine,
till all this earthly part of me
glows with thy fire divine.
    —EDWIN HATCH

Two Hearing Hearts Are Better Than One

For where two or three are gathered in my name, I am there among them.
—MATTHEW 18:20

I 'm not sure I would have been able to discern my way through the dilemma without the help of my on-line support group. About ten years ago an unusual opportunity presented itself. The mother of one of the teens in my youth group was graduating from seminary and leaving the area right between Anna's junior and senior years. Anna wanted to finish up high school where she'd started it, and her mother wondered if Anna could live with me for the year. I had a special bond with Anna and cared deeply for her, but would I, as a single professional woman, be able to adjust my busy life enough to meet the needs of a seventeen-year-old? Was this some sort of call from God?

I've never been a parent. Babysitting is the closest I've ever come to caring for kids. I was a youth leader for a few years, but that isn't the same as being completely responsible for someone. I had way more questions than answers, and so I gathered a small community of on-line friends to help me think through the options and discern whatever call might be in that invitation.

I hadn't heard of the Quaker clearness committee at that point. The Quakers assemble them when someone needs help sorting through a question or issue. The committee members listen and ask questions that help the focus person look deeply into his or her heart to determine what God's calling is. They don't give advice or tell the focus person what to do. Their main task is to wait with the focus person until clarity emerges.

My on-line group operated remarkably like a clearness committee, even though we hadn't heard of it then. I began the on-line conversation by outlining what the question was and why I was both drawn to the opportunity and nervous about accepting it. Over the course of a month the five people who "listened" to me responded with their questions—ones that made me dig a little deeper for answers. They gave me factual information when I asked for it, since they were all parents. They reflected back to me what they thought they were hearing, or what they sensed about what I'd written. Throughout all of it I felt deeply heard. I gained a sense of the joys and also the real difficulties of what I was considering.

In the end, I decided that I wasn't called to be Anna's guardian, and so she instead lived with a couple that had teens of their own. I was sorry to make that decision, but I also felt sure that living together was the wrong choice for both of us. That clarity came from my band of hearing hearts gathered on-line. Their attentiveness, their willingness to ask good questions, their acknowledgment of my gifts and even of my legitimate concerns left me with a sense of peacefulness about my decision. Had I tried to find my way through without help, I would have agonized over it much longer and probably would have felt unsure of the answer, no matter what decision I had made.

Our hearts and minds are often cloudy in the midst of those big moments when the stakes seem high, and friends with hearing hearts are a great gift in the midst of them. They remind me a little of a cellular phone commercial that's been running on television. People with phones full of static have miscommunicated in funny ways, and the cellular phone guy—the one with the static-free one—comes to the rescue so their conversations will be clear in the future. Friends who have hearing hearts do the same as they listen, ask questions, and help us work through the static until the call from God becomes clear.

Who are the people in your own life who help you clear up the static when the call isn't clear? How have they done that for you?

Blest be the tie that binds
Our hearts in Christian love:
The fellowship of kindred minds
Is like to that above.
We share our mutual woes,
Our mutual burdens bear,

And often for each other flows
The sympathizing tear.
From sorrow, toil, and pain,
And sin we shall be free;
And perfect love and friendship reign
Through all eternity.
  —JOHANN GEORG NÄGELI

Holiness in the Oddest Places

> But where shall wisdom be found? And where is the place of understanding?
> —JOB 28:12

Contemporary storyteller and essayist Robert Fulghum tells the story of a man who went to visit his rabbi. The man was troubled because he only succeeded in about half of the tasks he set for himself. Much to the man's surprise, the rabbi referred him to a specific page of an almanac, where he found a listing of the batting averages of some of baseball's greatest hitters. The best batting average was Ty Cobb's—.367, or one hit every third time at bat. The confused man went back to his rabbi to discover the significance of the information, and the answer was simple. If Ty Cobb got a hit only once every third time at bat, the man wasn't doing so badly if he succeeded half (or 50 percent) of the time. "Theology is amazing," Fulghum concludes, "and holy books abound."[1]

Holy books do abound, and they don't always look like holy books on the cover. They aren't limited to the subjects of theology, spirituality, biblical studies, and the like.

They don't have to be books about discernment to help you become a better discerner. All they need to do is help you open your heart to the myriad ways in which God operates in the world.

In fact, there's one whole category of books that I find holy that usually surprises people. I have several shelves of murder mysteries in the religion section of my library at home. All of them feature religious characters or settings, and I long ago learned that they could be my teachers, just like my books in theology, spirituality, and biblical studies. If you think about it, mysteries as a genre are appropriate for exploring the great Mystery of God and faith. The characters in these books struggle with the boundaries of the sacred and the secular, just as I do. Though I've never come across a dead body or had to solve a crime, many of the questions and dilemmas faced by the characters in these stories are mine as well.

In one series, a monk struggles with his sense of being drawn to help his friend, the police chief, solve mysteries, and he worries that his adventures conflict with his call to a life of religious devotion. In another series of books, the main character, who is Orthodox Jewish, tries to keep their spiritual and dietary practices while living the busy life of a police detective. Although the specifics may differ from my life, the desire to keep God in the center of busy days that distract me from God is not all that different.

One of my favorite authors always places her murder mystery in the midst of spiritual community. Several series rely on the importance of discernment and listening as ways to unravel the mystery. Another routinely focuses on themes of God's justice, while others take on important theological questions. I used to think that reading these books was my version of reading "mind candy"—thoughtless reading just for entertainment. But over the years I've learned differently. These books often cause me to think about what I believe and practice in my faith.

A friend of mine finds that art does the same for her. Meditating on paintings, sculptures, and other objects opens up her heart and helps her think more clearly about her beliefs. Others find the same thing with movies or drama. As I write this, in fact, there are all sorts of new books being published about movies and faith.

Robert Fulghum was right: holy books do abound. So do holy paintings, movies, dramas, and television shows. Even holy music abounds. God can speak through all sorts of mediums, not just in books that have religious covers and titles. So keep your eyes and heart open next time you read the almanac or daily newspaper, or the next time you're at the theatre or an art museum. You never know what bit of holiness and wisdom might be lurking in unexpected places.

In what unusual or unexpected sources have you found holiness or wisdom?

In the silence of the stars,
In the quiet of the hills,
In the heaving of the sea,
  Speak, Lord.

In the stillness of this room,
In the calming of my mind,
In the longing of my heart,
  Speak, Lord.

In the voice of a friend,
In the chatter of a child,
In the words of a stranger,
  Speak, Lord.

In the opening of a book,
In the looking at a film,
In the listening to music,
  Speak, Lord.

For your servant listens.[2]
  —DAVID ADAM

Quiet the Hamsters

For God alone my soul waits in silence.
—Psalm 62:1

*W*e don't often hear about the Desert Mothers, but Syncletica of Palestine was one. She lived alone in the desert in a small cave for twenty-eight years until a monk named Silas accidentally came upon her. On really busy, noisy, and crowded days, I envy Syncletica's escape into extended silence. On calmer days, of course, twenty-eight years of utter solitude and silence seems rather daunting, and maybe a little crazy.

Still, I wonder what the silence of the desert was like for all of those years. Did it allow Syncletica to turn off the noise in her mind so she could really talk to and listen to God? "Interior silence renders possible our conversation with Jesus Christ," says *The Rule of Taizé*,[1] a contemporary guidebook for one monastic community. Was twenty-eight years long enough for Syncletica to stop talking, to still the chatter in her head, and find real silence—silence that was rich with God's presence? I certainly hope so.

When people first begin to practice silence, they often find it difficult to silence the chatter in their minds. Even those who have practiced it for years still find silence to be elusive some days. The days' unresolved issues and arguments rumble around in the mind, refusing to leave or even to take a break from rehearsing their complaints or desires. They are like hamsters jogging all night on a squeaky wheel. I want to run screaming to the hamster cage and remove the offending wheel, just to quiet the noise. At the least, I wish the hamster would oil the silly thing so it wouldn't squeak. I find it very difficult to hear anything God has to say when the hamster won't sleep.

Discernment is easier for me when silence is more abundant, but I only seem to find silence when I am willing to give up the reins of control. The hamster rehashes the day's events because she—and I—want to make them come out differently. And as long as I hang onto that desire, silence eludes me. To really let my soul rest in silence requires that I be willing to listen in a new way, that I be open to options and conclusions other than the ones the hamster and I are currently concocting. Perhaps that's why silence scares most people. We're afraid of what we might hear and what we might be asked to do.

Still, silence frees us from being responsible for everything, from having to make decisions, and knowing the right thing to do. Silence is God's gift of peace and rest for the soul, a cessation of "strain and stress," as the nineteenth-century poet John Greenleaf Whittier wrote. And silence is the place where I can finally listen, instead of talking all the time. I'm not sure I'm ready for twenty-eight years of silence, but I'm grateful for the tidbits I find when the hamster chooses to rest.

Is silence a gift or a threat for you? Why?

Unending Peace

Take me, Lord, from busy-ness
To the place of quietness
From the tumult without cease
Into your unending peace.
Help me then, my Lord, to see
What I am and ought to be.[2]
   —DAVID ADAM

Lectio: Resting in the Word

Begin this exercise by sitting quietly for a few moments, with your eyes open or closed—whichever works best to help you center your thoughts on where you are, rather than on the events of the day. Breathe deeply, and try to let the muscles of your body relax. When you are ready, open with this simple prayer:

> May the words of my mouth, and the meditations of my (our) heart(s) be acceptable to you, O God, my rock and my redeemer. Amen.

1. Read this text from the monastic guidebook *The Rule of the Society of St. John the Evangelist*. Read through it slowly, and simply listen to what it is saying. What is the overall message of this passage? Allow yourself to just absorb the passage in silence for a couple of minutes.

> "There are varieties of gifts, but the same Spirit." We will not all have the same ways of prayer, but we will be united in seeking to open our hearts to "know the love of Christ that surpasses knowledge, so that [we] may be filled with all the fullness of God." The focus of our meditation may be on the Word of God in Scripture or holy writings. We may use our imaginations to enter into the deep meaning of a scriptural story. Or in slow, reflective reading we may wait for the Spirit to alert us to the words or image which are to be the means of God's particular revelation to us on this day; "the Spirit of truth . . . will

take what is mine and declare it to you." Then meditation opens our minds and hearts, and our response to
God's gift and disclosure is kindled by the Spirit within
us. God may touch us through icons, images, and sym-
bols, impregnating our hearts with grace and furthering
our transformation "from one degree of glory to another."
Sometimes God's word is waiting to be heard in our cur-
rent experience. The call may be to sift through it in
company with Christ to see how he is at work in our lives
and where he is leading.[1]

2. Read the passage a second time. As you do, listen for a
    word or phrase that seems to be an instruction for you.
    Is there something that jumps out at you from the text
    that feels like God's instruction or guidance for your
    life? Make a note of that word or phrase if you wish,
    and quietly contemplate that instruction for a few min-
    utes before moving on.

3. Read the passage a third time. When you hear the pas-
    sage you focused on in the second reading, allow your-
    self to experience a sense of gratitude for God's guid-
    ance in the word or words that stood out for you. Rest
    in that sense of thankfulness for a few minutes.

4. Read the passage a fourth time. Do you hear a word or
    phrase that calls you to confession? Notice what you
    are feeling at this time, and respond to God as appro-
    priate.

5. Read the passage a final time, and listen for an overall sense of guidance in the text. Find an image in your mind or in the words themselves that allows you to rest in God's guidance, even if you are not sure what God is asking of you.

If you are doing this exercise by yourself, you may wish to take a few minutes at the end of it and make some notes about your experiences and feelings while doing this. If you are doing this exercise with others, the group may find it helpful to allow some time for those who wish to share their thoughts and feelings.

Wisdom from Without

DAY 15

Pockets of Trust and Surrender

Father, if you are willing, remove this cup from me; yet, not my will but yours be done.

—LUKE 22:42

Contemporary writer Anne Lamott identifies herself as "someone who is perhaps *ever* so slightly more anxious than the average hypochondriac."[1] And because her father died of a malignant melanoma, she is more than a little vigilant when it comes to the moles of her body. They usually turn out to be nothing of consequence, but even a frown from her dermatologist and the suggestion that one be removed and biopsied puts her in a tailspin. In the midst of one of these episodes, as she worried about going to heaven and being put in a bad room with the other hysterics, she suddenly remembered that she believed in God. So, on a scrap of paper she wrote, "I am a little anxious. Help me remember that you are with me even now. I am going to take my sticky fingers off the control panel until I hear from you,"[2] and then she put the note into a drawer of the table next to her bed. Lamott was working on surrendering her own anxieties to God's will for her, even if God's will meant death.

Maybe you've done something like this at a retreat or prayer service. It seems to be common practice to ask participants in one of these events to list the burdens they want to shed on a piece of paper, pray to God to take those burdens or sins, and then destroy the papers, as if God magically removes them from our souls as we burn or rip the papers up. There's some sound theology behind that exercise, but in my experience, it often creates the expectation that our surrender of these sins or burdens or whatever we've listed will be gone now, once and forever, and that rarely happens. Maybe a portion of our burden is lifted—maybe it loses a few ounces in overall weight—and that's good. But for most of us, surrender isn't a once-and-for-all thing.

But discernment—and accepting God's call—requires some level of surrender from us. That, in turn, requires trust. But neither the trust nor the surrender comes all at once, as the practice of throwing your burdens into the fire might imply. Most of us can't let go that easily. We let go of the controls little by little, a few ounces or pounds at a time.

So I was grateful to Lamott for being really truthful about that as she continued her story of trying to surrender to whatever God had in mind for her. Her story has been mine as well:

> A grown up sort of peace came over me. I could feel it in the ensuing days, existing side by side with a heightened

sense of symptoms. I developed pain in my upper jaw, which made me wonder what I would look like with most of my jaw removed like poor old Sigmund Freud, and then a burning spot in my stomach, which filled my head with scenes in which I was heroically full of good humor after the colostomy. But in between symptoms I felt pockets of trust and surrender, as if I had gone into total free fall and then landed gently after a drop of just a foot and a half.[3]

Pockets of trust and surrender. . . . That sounds about right to me. Maybe someday Anne Lamott and I will find more than pockets, or maybe the pockets will just get larger so they hold more. Maybe she and I will be more able to surrender ourselves to God's desires for us without reservation. But for now, pockets are good enough. Small as they are, I think they please God.

Can you think of a moment when you gave up trying to control the world around you, even for a few moments? What was it like?

Open my eyes that I may see,
Incline my heart that I may desire,
Order my steps that I may follow
The way of your commandments.
  —LANCELOT ANDREWES

DAY 16

Seeing Yourself as God Sees You

She stood behind him at his feet, weeping, and began to bathe his feet with her tears and to dry them with her hair. Then she continued kissing his feet and anointing them with the ointment. Now when the Pharisee who had invited him saw it, he said to himself, "If this man were a prophet, he would have known who and what kind of woman this is who is touching him—that she is a sinner."

—Luke 7:38–39

The Pharisee thought he had caught Jesus in a trap. "If you were really a prophet," said the Pharisee under his breath to himself, "you would know what kind of woman it is who kisses your feet and anoints them, and you would not let her touch you that way." But Jesus knows that she is a prostitute and, as usual, tells a story that forces the Pharisee to rethink things. This outcast woman has been far more hospitable than Jesus' proper-minded hosts. She, who is supposed to be the scum of the earth, has bathed, dried, and kissed Jesus' feet, while the legalistic

Pharisee has neglected Jesus. The unnamed woman isn't afraid to show love for Jesus, while the invited guests and the host offer Jesus none of the usual hospitality. Though she has much for which she needs to be forgiven, Jesus sees something in her that the others have failed to see—something that even she failed to see in herself. Jesus saw into her heart and knew her for what she truly was. And he restored her to wholeness, just as God does for each of us. Being restored to wholeness—by seeing ourselves as God sees us—is both the risk and the joy of discernment.

The woman who washed Jesus' feet must have felt a little like the children's fairy tale ugly duckling did when the swans welcomed him and he knew what he was for the first time. All of her life she'd known herself through the eyes of a society that despised her, and now here was Jesus telling her that she was a whole different person from the one they—or she—knew. Jesus gave this woman one of those "aha" moments in discernment—that instant when she suddenly understood that reality isn't what she thought it was, and she was invited to hear a new reality with her heart. Perhaps more than anything, Jesus invited her to know herself as God's beloved, as someone God called to grow and change, instead of knowing herself as someone despised by society. Sometimes I wish we knew a bit more of her story following Jesus' defense of her in front of the Pharisees. Did she blossom like the ugly duckling/swan? Seeing an image of herself in Jesus' eyes that was completely new and alien to her, did she respond and become what God called her to be? What kind of courage does it take to believe what someone else—or what God—tells us, and allow our self-image to change and grow? For most of us it takes lots.

If I'd been that woman, I would have been quaking in my sandals. Jesus told her to go and sin no more. In other words, he told her to give up what was probably her only source of income. How did he expect her to live if she gave up prostitution? At the same time, he invited her to accept the gift of seeing herself differently—to see herself as the loving and caring human being he saw. How do you choose between a roof over your head with food on the table and a call to an unknown future, even when it's God's call to wholeness? The choices we have to make when we open our heart to hearing God's call are rarely that drastic, but you never know what's going to happen when you let God show you who you really are. You may discover you are a swan and not an ugly duckling, and that makes all the difference in the world to the call you'll hear and be able to accept.

If God put a mirror in front of you that offered a true reflection of who you are, what do you think you would see?

O God, by whom the meet are guided in judgment, and light rises up in darkness for the godly; give us, in all our doubts and uncertainties the grace to ask what thou wouldst have us do; that the spirit of wisdom may save us from false choices, and that in thy light we may see light and in thy straight paths may not stumble; through Jesus Christ our Lord.
—WILLIAM BRIGHT

Consult the Truth Tellers

Amazing grace! How sweet the sound that saved a wretch like me!
I once was lost but now am found, was blind but now I see.
—JOHN NEWTON "AMAZING GRACE"

A passenger cruising on an ocean liner couldn't find his room one day and was searching the decks looking for it. Finally he came across one of the boat's crew members and asked for help. The steward was glad to help and asked the man for his room number. "I couldn't tell you," replied the lost man, "but I'd know it at once because it had a lighthouse outside the porthole."[1]

That's a funny story in part because of its absurdity. But there are times when soul friends—our companions on the boat ride of life—can help us find our way out of some deep confusion that's not unlike this passenger's. Tom Wingo has to do that for his sister, Savannah, in the movie *The Prince of Tides*. Savannah has attempted suicide yet again, and her new psychiatrist, Susan Lowenstein, can't figure out what has damaged her so deeply. Lowenstein calls in Savannah's brother, Tom, to sort through the family history. Together, they work backwards in time until Tom remembers a childhood moment of severe trauma—one the family hasn't spoken of since it happened, and one that damaged every family member, particularly Savannah. Tom has held the memory for her all these years, because Savannah can't bear it, and as her brother—and soul friend, he tells the story to someone who can help Savannah heal.

We're rarely as confused in the discernment process as the passenger on the ocean liner. And neither are we usually in quite as much need of help as Savannah Wingo. Still, spiritual companions and soul friends can be important truth tellers for us when we're really turned around. True soul friends are listeners first and longest, but they're not afraid to help when they're needed. They're willing to tell us that we're completely confused, that we'll never find our cabin if we keep looking for a view left behind hours ago. Maybe they go to the main office, find our cabin number, and show us how to keep track of it and find it again. A good soul friend is willing to hold on to a hard truth but tell it at the appropriate moment—when it can be heard, digested, and used. And, as Tom did with his sister, they sit with us and support us as we absorb the truth and find the courage to heal or act on it as God wants us to.

The truth tellers in my own life haven't always been rewarded for their loyalty. It can be hard to hear the truth, to find out that I've been completely wrong, turned around, or confused, that I haven't been hearing with my heart. But I've usually come around in time and recognized that they speak out of love and the desire that I experience the life that God desires for me. God bless the soul friends who see clearly and aren't afraid to tell the truth at the right moment.

───────────────────────────────

How have the truth tellers in your own life affected your ability to discern what God calls you to do or be?

If I am right, thy Grace impart
   Still in the right to stay:
If I am wrong, oh teach my heart
   To find that better way.
   —ALEXANDER POPE

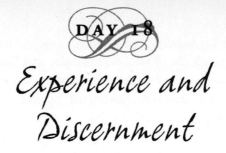

Experience and Discernment

O LORD, how manifold are your works! In wisdom you
have made them all; the earth is full of your creatures.
—PSALM 104:24

*C*ducation is experience," Merlin told his pupil, Wart,
the future King Arthur.[1] And with that, Merlin turned
Wart into a fish. The world looked entirely different from
a perch's perspective. Gravity, as humans know it, was no
longer a factor. And without legs, swimming required
entirely different kinds of movement from those a boy
made. Wart had to figure out how to move not only forward and backward but also up and down. He almost got
eaten by a bigger fish but was saved by Merlin at the last
moment. Wart also discovered that what he, as a boy, knew
about swans was just plain wrong. A swan that Wart had
thought of as deformed, one that he thought could paddle
with only one leg, gave him a rude reply: "Nonsense," said
the swan snappily. . . . "Swans like to rest in this position,
and you can keep your fishy sympathy to yourself."[2] His
perspective as a boy standing on the shore turned out to be
completely wrong.

I doubt that any of us will be fortunate enough to have Wart's experiences, but perhaps we can learn from the advice another teacher gave to his student in a story told by Catholic priest and contemporary writer Edward Hays. Before accepting any new students, the teacher in Hays's parable required each prospective student to submit to a medical exam given by the teacher.[3] "Soul-dead" was the diagnosis for one aspiring student. "I'm sorry," said the teacher, "but without a soul it would be a waste of your time and mine for you to become a student of the spiritual path."[4] The shocked aspiring student protested that Plato said the soul was immortal, so how could he be soul-dead. Western philosophy had nothing to do with the condition, according to the teacher, but if the student wanted to enliven his soul again there was a solution: "Leave the city at once and go to the nearest forest or wilderness area you can find. Camp out there without a tent, sleeping bag, port-a-potty, clock, radio or other modern comforts. Stay there day and night until the trees, wild grasses, birds, wild creatures and even the bugs begin to talk to you."[5]

The teacher's advice was the next-best thing to having a Merlin to turn you into a fish or bird or rock. When was the last time you took enough time, and focused clearly enough, to let the wild grasses speak to you? The idea that animals and even inanimate objects have something to teach is a foreign one in Western culture. But everything that exists reflects its Maker and so has something to teach us about the desires of God. Each responds to the forces around it in some unique way and has something to tell us about how we might understand and respond to the forces—to God's forces—around us.

The tall wild grasses display flexibility in the face of even the strongest winds. Rocks, once jagged, become smooth after years of being washed by the waves. Plants grow and die according to their seasons. I haven't quite figured out what mosquitoes have to teach me yet, but I'm sure there's a lesson there somewhere. It probably has something to do with persistence.

Book learning is wonderful and exciting, and far be it from me—as an author and editor—to suggest that you dispense with what you can learn from books. But study involves picking our noses up out of the books sometimes and paying attention to what the beings and objects around us have to teach as well. To know God well, to understand God's desires for our world, it is necessary to seek out experiences beyond what books can teach. Education is experience, as Merlin told Wart. I doubt that there is anything in the world that cannot be a teacher for us if we truly pay attention, even to that pesky mosquito.

What wisdom might a plant, animal, or other natural object impart to you that could illuminate your own discernment right now?

Holy Spirit:
As the wind is your symbol, so forward our goings.
As the dove so launch us heavenwards.
As water so purify our spirits.
As a cloud so abate our temptations.
As dew so revive our languor.
As fire so purge out our dross.
     —CHRISTINA ROSSETTI

Examining the Heart

Create in me a clean heart, O God, and put a new and right spirit within me.

—PSALM 51:10

*I*t is important to tell at least from time to time the secret of who we truly and fully are," writes popular author Frederick Buechner, "even if we tell it only to ourselves— because otherwise we run the risk of losing track of who we truly and fully are and little by little come to accept instead the highly edited version which we put forth in hope that the world will find it more acceptable than the real thing."[1] Buechner goes on to tell the story of his mother, who found his autobiographical writing unacceptable. Early in what became a prolific writing career, Buechner fictionalized the story of his father's suicide. His mother, furious with what she considered to be his betrayal of a family secret, never read another one of his books. She didn't want to know what he was saying; she preferred her own highly edited version of her son's and her own life.

Most of us are more like Buechner's mother than not, at least with some part of our lives. There are episodes we colorize, as they do with the old black-and-white movies, in order to make them (ourselves, actually) more attractive. Once that's done, we try to avoid contact with anyone or anything that might spoil our carefully crafted masterpiece. Unfortunately, it is hard to avoid God, who knows the real story. David tried it, according to the story of David and Bathsheba in 2 Samuel, and he was no more successful that we will be.

David coveted Bathsheba, the wife of Uriah, slept with her, and impregnated her. In order to cover up—to colorize—what he'd done, he had Uriah killed in battle, and then David married Bathsheba in order to make the story come out right. So God sent Nathan to David, with a story of a great injustice that inflamed David, until he realized that Nathan's story was actually about David's misdeeds.

David needed a Nathan to help him see that he wasn't paying attention to his own life and whether it fit with God's desires. But there's an ancient prayer practice that you and I can use if we want to avoid the embarrassment of dealing with a Nathan. The Prayer of *Examen,* a simple prayer for exploring one's conscience at any given point of time, is also a prayer that helps us learn to discern God's presence in our daily lives. It is a prayer that helps us be truthful with God, instead of trying to tell God the edited version of our lives. The prayer considers two simple questions: How did you move toward what God is calling you to be or do today (or this week, or month)? and In what ways did you move away from God's call today? When you first start using the prayer, it may be hard to recount any of the ways that you moved toward or away from God. But with practice, you begin to notice the movements more easily. And once you begin to be familiar with the way you and God work together, discernment becomes much easier, and the need for a highly edited version of your life becomes less necessary—especially in your time with God.

When you reflect back on your day, what moments or activities can you identify that were movements in accord with God's desires for you? What moments or activities can you identify that seemed to be movements away from God?

Almighty God who hast sent the Spirit of truth unto us to guide us into all truth: so rule our lives by thy power that we may be truthful in thought and word and deed. May no fear or hope ever make us false in act or speech; cast out from us whatsoever loveth or maketh a lie, and bring us all into the perfect freedom of thy truth; through Jesus Christ our Lord.

DAY 20

The Blessing of Friends

Do not judge, so that you may not be judged.
—MATTHEW 7:1

With friends like Job's, as the old saying goes, who needs enemies? There was poor Job, who had lost most of what he held dear, and along come his three so-called friends to rub salt in his wounds. In their minds Job's suffering was proof enough that he'd sinned against God. The appearance of being punished was all they needed to declare him guilty.

Then there are friends like Abba Sisoes, one of the Desert Fathers who lived in the fourth century. A troubled man sought him out and told the Desert Father of his desire to seek revenge on a brother who had hurt him. Abba Sisoes tried to dissuade the seeker from avenging himself and to leave judgment to God, but the man was not persuaded. So Abba Sisoes invited the man to pray with him: "God, we no longer need you to care for us, since we do justice for ourselves."[1] The seeker instantly realized his error and asked forgiveness of the Desert Father.

Sisoes knew how to be a good spiritual companion. Instead of blaming, judging, or lecturing endlessly, Sisoes accepted what the man seeking help told him and gently

showed him the consequences of his thinking and suggested possible action. Sisoes didn't tie the man up and prevent
him from acting against his advice. He didn't lecture the
seeker for days. He didn't adopt a self-righteous tone of
voice and insist that only he knew the truth. Abba Sisoes
accepted that the offended man could see no other path for
the moment and allowed him the freedom to choose that
path if he wished, but he gently offered him a glimpse of
another possible approach to the situation. And because
Sisoes wasn't intent on having his own way, the seeker was
freed to consider the Abba's suggestion and vision.

Acting as Sisoes did is hard work, and I'm always
grateful for friends who can manage it. I'm equally grateful
when I remember to hold my tongue and leave those I care
about to choose the path that seems right to them. I have a
friend who is struggling to extricate himself from a difficult
situation right now, and the answer looks so clear to me
most of the time. But I've been in his shoes, and I remember how hard it is to walk away from something that used
to nurture you but no longer does so. It's natural to hope
that things will turn around and return to normal.
Sometimes they do. Often they don't. But my friend will
know when the time is right to leave or recommit to staying. And in the meantime, I'm working hard to keep my
mouth shut and my heart and ears open. I don't know how
God and my friend will work this one out. My role is just
to sit and be present instead of judging my friend. That's
hard enough work for me. I'll leave the rest to God.

Who have been the special friends in your life who have listened to you without judging you? How have they influenced your discernment in situations in the past?

Almighty God, and most merciful Father, who has given us a new commandment that we should love one another, give us also grace that we may fulfill it. Make us gentle, courteous, and forbearing. Direct our lives so that we may look each to the good of the other in word and deed. And hallow all our friendships by the blessing of your Spirit, for his sake who loves us and gave himself for us, Jesus Christ our Lord.

—BROOKE FOSS WESCOTT

DAY 21

Wise Guides

In every generation [Wisdom] passes into holy souls and makes them friends of God, and prophets.
—WISDOM OF SOLOMON 7:27

I'd never seen sheep tethered together before. A few years ago on a visit to Ireland I saw lots of pairs of sheep joined by short ropes. I was told that this prevented the sheep from jumping over the low stone fences that surrounded their grazing areas. The two sheep, tied together, simply couldn't coordinate their efforts enough to jump the fence at the same time. Theirs was an odd sort of intimacy. They were together all the time but they were a noose around each other's neck as well, limiting each other's moves and abilities.

If those sheep had been people bound together, they wouldn't have made very good soul friends. I know because I've seen people hold each other back just as those sheep did. A woman I knew once made a habit of befriending people who were experiencing some sort of trouble in their life. She had a sort of radar that zeroed in on people who were happy to be totally dependent on her, at least for a while. She spent all sorts of time with them, opened her house to them, and helped them in any way she could. But the moment these people began to stand on their own two feet and push for a little independence, she turned on them and shooed them out of her life. She needed to be the center of their existence, and if they wanted to jump the fence without her, she turned her back on them and terminated the friendship.

Good spiritual guides respond differently from that. They're a little more like Obiwan Ben Kenobi was with Luke Skywalker in the *Star Wars* movies. Ben knows who—and whose—Luke is when they first meet. In fact, he knows more than Luke does at that point. So Ben began to tell Luke the truth, little by little, but he never forced Luke into any direction. He let Luke figure it out for himself. When Ben suggested that Luke help him deliver critical plans against the evil Alliance to the Rebels, Luke said no. And Ben let him go gracefully, saying that Luke must do what he felt was right.

Later, when Luke joined Ben in delivering the plans, Ben taught Luke to begin using the powers—the gifts—that lay dormant in Luke. Ben instructed him in the art of using "the Force"—to feel it deeply within himself, to stretch out with his feelings to make things happen. Ben was wise in ways that good spiritual guides are, and, like other wise guides, he knew how easily we can fool ourselves. "Your eyes can fool you," said Ben, as he blindfolded Luke temporarily. With Luke blindfolded, Ben taught him to reach deep inside himself and align himself with the Force. Ben knew, too, when it was time for Luke to follow his own path, even though that path diverged from Ben's.

These are the kind of spiritual companions you'll need in the discernment process. Good guides help you name and claim your gifts. They stand by you and encourage you to look deep inside for God's call, and then follow that call, even when it takes you away from them. True and faithful guides help you hear and respond to God's call more deeply with your heart, rather than tether themselves to you. They delight in seeing you jump over the fence, with or without them.

❧ ————————————————————————————

Who have been the wise guides in your own life?

Blessed are You, God of Unity,
        for entering our lives through friendship.
Make us, we pray, worthy of such a gift
        by being faithful but non-possessive,
        by being loyal but honest
        and by being ever grateful
        for the gift of good friends.
Blessed are You, Lord our God,
        who gifts us with the joys of friendship.[1]
    —EDWARD HAYS

Lectio: Resting in the Word

Begin this exercise by sitting quietly for a few moments, with your eyes open or closed—whichever works best to help you center your thoughts on where you are, rather than on the events of the day. Breathe deeply, and try to let the muscles of your body relax. When you are ready, open with this simple prayer:

> May the words of my mouth, and the meditations of my (our) heart(s) be acceptable to you, O God, my rock and my redeemer. Amen.

1. Read this text from Acts 9 through slowly, and simply listen to the story. What is happening here? What is the overall message of this passage? Allow yourself to just absorb the story in silence for a couple minutes.

> Now as [Saul] was going along and approaching Damascus, suddenly a light from heaven flashed around him. He fell to the ground and heard a voice saying to him, "Saul, Saul, why do you persecute me?" He asked, "Who are you, Lord?" The reply came, "I am Jesus, whom you are persecuting. But get up and enter the city, and you will be told what you are to do." Saul got up from the ground, and though his eyes were open, he could see nothing; so [his traveling companions] led him by the hand and brought him into Damascus.
>
> Now there was a disciple in Damascus named Ananias. The Lord said to him in a vision, "Ananias." He

answered, "Here I am, Lord." The Lord said to him, "Get up and go to the street called Straight, and at the house of Judas look for a man of Tarsus named Saul. At this moment he is praying, and he has seen in a vision a man named Ananias come in and lay his hands on him so that he might regain his sight." But Ananias answered, "Lord, I have heard from many about this man, how much evil he has done to your saints in Jerusalem; and here he has authority from the chief priests to bind all who invoke your name." But the Lord said to him, "Go, for he is an instrument whom I have chosen to bring my name before Gentiles and kings and before the people of Israel; I myself will show him how much he must suffer for the sake of my name."

So Ananias went and entered the house. He laid his hands on Saul and said, "Brother Saul, the Lord Jesus, who appeared to you on your way here, has sent me so that you may regain your sight and be filled with the Holy Spirit." And immediately something like scales fell from his eyes, and his sight was restored. (Portions of Acts 9:2–18)

2.   Read the passage a second time. As you do, listen for a word or phrase that seems to be an instruction for you. Is there something that jumps out at you from the text that feels like God's instruction or guidance for your life? Make a note of that word or phrase, if you wish, and quietly contemplate that instruction for a few minutes before moving on.

3. Read the passage a third time. When you hear the passage you focused on in the second reading, allow yourself to experience a sense of gratitude for God's guidance in the word or words that stood out to you. Rest in that sense of thankfulness for a few minutes.

4. Read the passage a fourth time. Do you hear a word or phrase that calls you to confession? Notice what you are feeling at this time, and respond to God as appropriate.

5. Read the passage a final time, and listen for an overall sense of guidance in the text. Find an image in your mind or in the words themselves that allows you to rest in God's guidance, even if you are not sure what God is asking of you.

If you are doing this exercise by yourself, you may wish to take a few minutes at the end of it and make some notes about your experiences and feelings while doing this. If you are doing this exercise with others, the group may find it helpful to allow some time for those who wish to share their thoughts and feelings.

Practicing the Presence of God

DAY 22

Just Keep Trying

For now we see in a mirror, dimly, but then we will see face to face. Now I know only in part; then I will know fully, even as I have been fully known.

—1 CORINTHIANS 13:12

I admit it. Sometimes—even often—the spiritual masters whose books I read intimidate me. In *The Practice of the Presence of God,* seventeenth-century monk Brother Lawrence writes about how he focuses on God while working in the kitchen, repairing shoes, or whatever other task he is assigned. He even records that he "was more united to God in his ordinary activities than when devoting himself to religious activities which left him with a profound spiritual dryness."[1] To me, that statement feels a little like he is boasting. I want to scream, "Get real!" at him sometimes. But perhaps that's just my envy showing.

Then there's a contemporary master of the art of attention, the Buddhist monk Thich Nhat Hanh, who teaches us how to wash dishes or eat a tangerine focusing all our attention on what we are doing at the moment rather than thinking about future moments. In his book *Anger: Wisdom for Cooling the Flames,* he even advises us to practice mindfulness—paying attention—by chewing each

87

mouthful of food fifty times before swallowing.[2] Try it some time. That's a lot of attention to pay to a mouthful of corn flakes.

These two men, and others like them, sometimes leave me with a feeling of deep spiritual incompetence. They speak with such assurance and ease about being attentive, or mindful, as Thich Nhat Hanh would say, and I have a sense that the bar has been set too high for me. I forget that they weren't born knowing how to be so attentive, so attuned to the Source of all wisdom. Fortunately, Brother Lawrence, while he sets the bar too high for me to reach, also lets me off the hook by reminding me that "in the beginning a persistent effort is needed to form the habit of continually talking with God and to refer all we do to Him but that after a little care His love brings us to it without difficulty."[3] The bar comes down a few notches—thank goodness.

It is so easy to read the words of those who tell us to be attentive to our bodies, our dreams, our heart's desires, the story of our life—to do all the things that make us better discerners—and to think that the writer, our spiritual companion for the moment, has mastered wisdom we can never hope to attain. Perhaps, occasionally, that's true, but my own experience tells me that it isn't always so. I write about things I have experienced and understand to be true and wise, but I make no pretense of telling you that I am able to practice them all the time. I struggle with them just as Brother Lawrence did in the beginning. My experience is the same as his—that practice increases my ability to observe and hear with the heart. I glimpsed God's presence and guidance only out of the corner of my eye when I first began my conscious spiritual journey. I notice God more often now, and I've learned to attend to God's presence in more ways than I knew existed ten years ago. God willing, in ten more years, I will be more attentive than I am today.

I don't know if practice makes perfect because I haven't done anything perfectly in my life thus far. But I do know that practice improves us and our abilities—that continuing to try to pay attention more regularly during each day actually helps me be more attentive and more discerning as the years move along. What I saw only dimly some years ago is a bit clearer today. I'll bet that's true for you, too.

In what ways have you grown in your ability to sense God's presence and guidance over the years?

Creating God, in you we live and move and have our being: We humbly pray you so to guide and govern us by your Holy Spirit, that in all the cares and occupations of our life we may not forget you, but may remember that we are ever walking in your sight; through Jesus Christ our Lord. Amen.
—THE BOOK OF COMMON PRAYER

Play and Pray

I, God, am your playmate! I will lead the child in you in
wonderful ways, for I have chosen you.[1]
—MECHTILD OF MAGDEBURG

*H*er language—her words about, to, and from God—
are so surprising that it almost shocks me into a new
understanding about God. I don't know about you, but I
don't usually think of myself as God's playmate. No one
ever taught me to imagine myself as sitting on the floor
with God building castles with blocks, but maybe they
should have. Maybe that's exactly what discernment is like.

Mechtild's chats with God were full of playfulness.
This thirteenth-century mystic recorded her delightful and
intimate conversations for us to listen in on. "Woman, you
must adorn yourself," she wrote, recording one such conversation with God. "Maiden, you ought to dance merrily,
dance like my elected one! Dance like the noblest, loveliest,
richest Queen."[2] Now we're not only building castles, but
also dancing with God. Heady stuff.

But maybe Mechtild is onto something here. We talk
about and approach discerning God's guidance with so
much seriousness. That's probably appropriate. Reverence
for God always is. But God also seems to enjoy playfulness,

even in the midst of discernment. Look at the story of young Samuel in 1 Samuel 3.

Samuel was doing his job in the temple and minding his own business. One night while he was resting he heard a voice calling out his name. He made the natural assumption that his teacher Eli was calling, and he responded. But no, Eli hadn't called Samuel. Probably a bit baffled, Samuel went back to his mat to rest. The voice came again: "Samuel!" Well, you know the story. This happened three times before Eli realized that God was calling Samuel, and he instructed Samuel to answer God next time he heard the voice. But think about it. God could easily have let Samuel know that it was God who was calling him the first time. It was a little as if God stood behind Samuel, off to the left side, and reached around to tap him on the right shoulder. Samuel looks right, of course, and finds nothing there. God had so much fun with this little joke that God tried it a few more times. Poor Samuel might have looked the wrong way all night if it hadn't been for Eli's help.

This practical joke of God's was the prelude to God's telling Samuel what was to come, what God was going to do next. Playfulness was the prelude to discernment for Samuel. Maybe it can be that way for us, too. I wonder if we're not just a little more receptive to God's desires and dreams when we're feeling loose and relaxed, even when we're laughing. I know I'm more creative when I'm in a playful mood, when I stop taking the world so seriously and just let my natural energy and enthusiasm have free reign. Maybe we need to just lighten up a little if we want to know God's desires for us and the world around us and trust that Mechtild's reporting of God's words to her are words for us as well. God, our playmate, will lead the child in us in wonderful ways, for God has chosen us. Hallelujah, and yippee!

In what playful activity or activities that you enjoy do you have a sense of God's presence?

I cannot dance, O Lord,
unless you lead me.
If you will that I leap joyfully
then you must be the first to dance and sing![3]
    —MECHTILD OF MAGDEBURG

Discernment When God Is AWOL

My God, my God, why have you forsaken me? Why are you so far from helping me, from the words of my groaning? O my God, I cry by day, but you do not answer; and by night, but find no rest.

—PSALM 22:1–2

"My God, my God, why have you forsaken me?" In the Gospels of Matthew and Mark these were the last words Jesus uttered from the cross. Shortly after he said them he breathed his last and died. I shudder to think of how lonely that moment must have been. I can't even imagine the pain of it, nor do I really want to. I've never experienced the kind of pain and abandonment Jesus must have felt on the cross, but there have been times in my own life when the Light was eclipsed, when God seemed to be AWOL for long periods of time. For days, weeks, or months, my heart listened, but there didn't seem to be anything to hear.

A friend of mine who attends a mainline church today sometimes laments that she misses the strong presence of God that she found in a charismatic church she attended years ago. Her experience of a charismatic church was that people *expected* God to be present and that people would be healed during the worship time, and often their expectations were met. Sometimes we bring those same kinds of feelings to the practice of discernment. We assume that if our hearts are open God will automatically speak to us and tell us all we need to know to move forward on our journey. We've read all these biblical accounts of other people's "successful" moments of discernment, and we expect the same to happen to us. Sometimes those expectations are helpful in actually opening our hearts to God's desires. But when Moses' burning bush doesn't appear on schedule, God feels absent and uncaring. There are, however, lots of reasons for feeling that God is AWOL.

I've also found that sometimes God is talking very loudly and clearly in response to my query but that when I'm not overly fond of the answer I'm hearing, it is easier for me to convince myself that God isn't really communicating with me. Invariably I "wake up" one day and realize that God's been talking nonstop to me; I've just had my hands over my ears and heart, trying to keep God out.

Sometimes being unable to hear God is just a matter of fatigue or illness or something else we can't solve or control at the moment. I don't know if there are just times when God wants us to rest, relax, or recover, and God metaphorically turns off the light for a while and suggests that we nap, but that's what it feels like. For whatever reason, the time isn't right for discernment, and nothing we can do changes that. The time for discernment will return when God senses that we are renewed and ready, and not a moment before.

Though God feels absent in all of these times, God is never absent from our lives, never uninterested in our journey. It feels that way sometimes, but the One who formed us in our mother's womb remains with us always, even if silently at times. So scream, argue, rest, recover, or do whatever else you need to do when God seems to be incommunicado. But do it with the certain knowledge that God hears you and will respond, even if it feels like you're talking to thin air for now.

What have been the reasons that God felt AWOL in your own life at times?

God, where are you?
I beg, I plead . . . and you do not answer.
I shout, I yell . . . and get nothing.
Break your silence, O God.
Speak to me!
Teach me!
Rebuke me!
Strike me down!
But do not remain silent.
The God who is mute. Is that who you are?
You have revealed yourself as the speaking God—our communicating Cosmos.

You pointed Abraham to a city whose builder and maker was God.

You revealed your divine name to Moses.

You spoke with clarity
to David,
to Ruth,
to Esther,
to Isaiah,
to Ezekiel,
to Daniel,
to Mary,
to Paul,
and a host of others.

Why are the heavens made of iron for me?

Job, I know, experienced you as the hidden God. And Elijah held a lonely vigil over earthquake, wind, and fire. Me too.

O God of wonder and of mystery, teach me by means of your wondrous, terrible, all-embracing silence.

Amen.[1]

　　—RICHARD FOSTER

DAY 25

A Little Reason, a Little Imagination

But where shall wisdom be found? And where is the place of understanding?

—JOB 28:12

Reason and imagination don't seem like close companions. When was the last time someone told you to be reasonable and imaginative at the same time? But if you want to hear well and clearly with the heart, you'll need to befriend both reason and imagination. One without the other doesn't work, as the stories of Job and John illustrate.

Job was a reasonable man. All he wanted of God was for God to be reasonable as well. In the midst of loss and suffering Job wanted an explanation from God. He wanted to be proven innocent at a trial. He wanted an explanation—a logical and reasonable one—for his suffering, or he wanted to be relieved of it. Even Job's so-called friends sought reasonable explanations for Job's misfortune.

God wasn't very obliging about a reasonable answer, however, and thousands of years later we're still trying to figure out what God really meant. "Where were you when I laid the foundation of the earth? Tell me, if you have understanding," God commands Job (Job 38:4). And then God listed lots of items in creation that Job couldn't explain, any more than we can. Reason is useless, or at least limited, for understanding why the world is the way it is. We have to use our imagination to cobble together some explanation that helps us get through the day.

John, on the other hand, lived in the world of imagination without the benefit of reason. John is the main character in the recent movie, *A Beautiful Mind,* and his condition was medical—he was a schizophrenic, so his story wasn't about God or discernment per se. But his story still illustrates what happens when reason disappears. John lived in an imaginary world when he wasn't on his medication, and he spent his time running away from dangers that didn't actually exist. He was terrorized by his own imagination and lacked the power of reason with which to see clearly. His wife, doctor, and friends had to work very hard to help John see what was reasonable or real. He had to work very hard on remaining reasonable and recognizing when imagination was totally taking over as well.

Both of these men struggled with an imbalance of reason and imagination—a temporary inability to use both to discern what was going on and what might be the way ahead. Most of us struggle to keep reason and imagination balanced, too. We tend to prefer one over the other, if just a little bit. I'd much rather have things just "come to me" via my imagination or intuition than sit down and actually plod through a list of reasons, a pro and con list. But time after time, I've discovered that imagination only takes me so far when I'm trying to figure out where God is guiding me, and that blasted list helps me understand a bit more. Friends of mine want to use their reason and have clear explanations about how and why God is guiding them in certain directions, and they're just as frustrated in coming to understanding that way as I am when I neglect to use reason at all.

Reason and imagination are the seesaw on which discernment hinges. Use one and not the other, and you're sitting on the ground, in the dirt, looking up at the other end of the seesaw, which is somewhere up in the air without you.

Which do you prefer to use, or use first: reason or imagination?

Lord, take, take my lips and speak through them, take my mind and think through it, take my heart and set it on fire for love of you.[1]
—ATTRIBUTED TO W. H. AITKEN

My Life Would Be Better If . . .

For where your treasure is, there your heart will be also.
—MATTHEW 6:21

Your Money or Your Life. That was the title of the book sitting on the shelf in front of me. You have choices to make, the book told me, and those choices have consequences. But the question is even larger than the title implies. At the core, the question is, What does your heart truly desire? What do you absolutely ache for in this life? Who does God call you to be? If you don't know, what's stopping you from listening? And if you do know what you desire—what God calls you to do or be—with every ounce of your being, what's preventing you from going after it?

For me, sorting out what I most want is difficult, particularly when many conflicting voices try to tell me what I *should* want. Television, radio, movies, newspapers, and magazines all say I should want to be romantically involved with someone, that I should be far more fit than I am, and that I should use all sorts of medicines to ensure that I never have a single uncomfortable moment. Clearly I'm missing all sorts of social events. I need new summer patio furniture and at least a hundred new plants for the garden, as well as new clothes and everything the local discount store can supply me with at any hour of the day or night. The number of messages taken in during a day—not to mention the number that don't register on a conscious level—is incredible, and by the end of most days I wonder whether the national economy rises and falls depending on my personal willingness to spend money. It takes very little effort to get caught up in thinking that these might be things I actually *need* to have, that owning all this stuff is what my heart desires.

It takes great effort some days to remember that I don't actually want or need many of these things. I wouldn't mind having a comfortable chair for my patio, but there's really not a whole lot else that I need. Even so, my heart doesn't ache with desire for a lawn chair. In a workshop I attended recently the speaker asked us to answer three questions without thinking about or analyzing our answers. The three questions were identical to each other. Three times he asked us to complete the sentence "My life would be better if . . ." Without a moment's hesitation, I recorded my desire to have more time to write and to lead retreats and workshops, and the need for more breathing and praying spaces in my life. If I'd thought about the question before responding, I probably wouldn't have answered in the same way, but the three things I wrote down really are my heart's desires—the things I most *need* right now, rather than what I might want, or what I think I am supposed to want.

And now, my task is to figure out how to make those things happen. I've got at least a dozen good reasons why I can't spend more time writing, teaching, and just being. My workload is heavy. People are counting on me to get things done. I've got a mortgage to pay. Those things matter; they're real. But at some level, they're also beside the point. I suspect that the things that my heart most desires, at least in this case, are the things God calls on me to be and do. They are the things that will make me of most service to others and probably the happiest I can be as well. So I continue to ponder my heart's desires and listen for their wisdom for my life. And I continue to look for ways to make them, instead of the workload and the mortgage payment, the daily reality of my existence.

Without thinking about it, what are three things that would improve your life?

O Lord, in whom is our hope, remove far from us, we pray thee, empty hopes and presumptuous confidence. Make our hearts so right with thy holy and loving heart, that hoping in thee we may do good; until that day when faith and hope shall be abolished by sights and possession, and love shall be all in all.
—CHRISTINA ROSSETTI

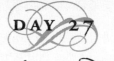

Waiting Rooms

Lead me in your truth, and teach me, for you are the
God of my salvation; for you I wait all day long.
—PSALM 25:5

spend a lot of time in waiting areas. Like most people, I
spend the requisite time waiting to see the doctor or den-
tist, or standing in line at the grocery store, but I also travel a lot, so I spend a lot of time waiting for airplanes, trains,
or buses. And because I spend a lot of time waiting, I've
watched a lot of people playing The Waiting Game.

Have you ever watched other people waiting? Some
are very relaxed. They bring a good book to read, or they
strike up a conversation with someone else who's waiting
too. In the airport or train station, some of the good waiters stretch their legs with a long walk down the terminal
and back, just to get a little exercise. If they're stuck in the
airport on Superbowl Sunday—something that happened
to me earlier this year, they head to the bar, grab a beer, and
enjoy rooting (loudly!) for their favorite team. Or they walk
the halls and look at the art exhibits. A few even visit the
airport chapel and enjoy some silent prayer time. Good
waiters relax and accept that they're going to wait for some

period of time, and they either just enjoy being low-key and quiet for a while, or they find some entertainment.

Then there are those who don't wait so comfortably. They can't seem to actually get a page of their book read because they're so distracted by the waiting or, God forbid, the delay. They exude an air of frustration and annoyance, and they sometimes take that out on the airline or train personnel. They spend a lot of time going from their seat to the monitor to check the latest on whether the plane or train is going to be on time, or just how late it's going to be. Some of them are on their cell phones complaining about their boredom to whoever the poor soul happens to be on the other end of the line, and the rest of us get to listen in too. Waiting seems like a personal insult to these folks, who exude the sense that they're being massively inconvenienced (which, sometimes, they are), or that they're too important to be kept in waiting mode.

Learning to hear with the heart is definitely an activity to avoid if you abhor waiting. God doesn't seem to have the same value system we have around the issues of time and efficiency. So if waiting makes you angry and frustrated all the time, you can probably find better things to do with your days and nights than practice discernment. Discernment calls for a bit of creative waiting, for being able to balance patience and impatience, for knowing and not knowing, with a little style. Creative waiting involves being engaged and attentive to your goal. It means tolerating a little boredom, anger, or fatigue when you can't figure out where God is guiding you at the moment. When the reception's lousy, the creative waiter takes a walk, gets some exercise, goes to look at something else—some art, a ball game, a movie—for a while. A friend of mine calls it "changing the channel," something we all need to do when the reception's poor or we can't understand what we're hearing—or not hearing—with our hearts.

"Lead me in your truth . . . for you I wait all day long," writes the Psalmist. And sometimes we wait for God not just all day long, but for a week, a month, or months on end. God's truth isn't always clear or obvious, any more than the satellite dish on the television is on a snowy day. But discernment is about waiting creatively for the static to clear, and it's about staying engaged and attentive—continuing to listen and talk with God, even on the days when it seems like it would be easier and more efficient to just take over and be God instead.

What kind of a waiter are you?

Set free, O Lord, the souls of your servants from all restlessness and anxiety. Give us that peace and power which flow from you. Keep us in all perplexity and distress, that upheld by your strength and stayed on the rock of your faithfulness we may abide in you now and evermore.

—Francis Paget

DAY 28

This Is Your Life

For it was you who formed my inward parts; you knit me together in my mother's womb. I praise you, for I am fearfully and wonderfully made.

—PSALM 139:13–14

When I was young, I watched a television show called *This Is Your Life.* Some unsuspecting person sat and listened as one voice after another from his or her past spoke to him or her from backstage. The voice could be anyone from the past: a third-grade school teacher, a next-door neighbor, a college roommate, an old girlfriend. One by one, the host of the show and these people from the past told stories that gave the audience some sense of what the person's life had been like, who they were. They created a picture, a collage, that showed you what path the person had taken and what the results had been. But I wonder if they were telling the story of this person's life the same way he or she would have told it. Or the same way God would have told it.

Wouldn't it be fascinating if we got to be the honored guest of the show, and God was the speaker from backstage? After all, God knows our lives so much better than any individual from our past or present. "O LORD, you have searched me and known me," writes the creator of Psalm 139. "You know when I sit down and when I rise up; you discern my thoughts from far away. You search out my path and my lying down, and are acquainted with all my ways. Even before a word is on my tongue, O LORD, you know it completely." God knows our life story. God helped write it and continues to do so.

I, for one, would like to hear God tell my story, if only to know if God and I would tell the story the same way. I'd like to have God tell me why some things happened as they did, why other things didn't happen, what God hopes will be the story of my future. I'd like God to be really clear about how God tried to move in my life, how I responded, and what happened as a result.

So far, however, God seems to want to leave the storytelling to me. So every once in a while I take some time to stop and reflect on the past and how my perspective has changed. At eighteen, I told the story of my life one way, and now, at forty-something, I think of it quite differently. Hindsight—the gift of all those people from the past on the television show—is marvelously helpful in clarifying our lives. The movement of God in my life yesterday is probably impossible for me to understand, much less articulate, but God's guidance to me over the last couple of decades seems a bit clearer. I have a sense of the ways in which God has drawn me along, encouraging and coaxing me in certain directions.

I can sense, as well, some of God's invitations that I haven't yet accepted, either out of my own stubbornness or fear or just out of lack of attention. In all likelihood, God is guiding me in ways that I'm not even noticing at all right now. Perhaps when I look back at my life today ten years from now, I'll have a completely new perspective and will tell the story in a whole new way. Maybe I won't even recognize the story as I tell it today.

For many years I had a spiritual director whose favorite question to me was, "And how do you sense God at work in the story you've just told me? What's the invitation here?" I don't always have the answer to that question. It's hard to pay attention to God at work in my life all the time. But those are always good questions to come back to from time to time. I suspect that I, or someone else, will ask them many more times before my time on earth is over. And I'll be curious to know what my answer is when it is asked next.

When you look back over your life, how do you see God's guidance at work?

God of power and presence,
you are the midwife of our lives,
always drawing us on to be born again,
encouraging, exhorting, calming,
containing even death.
You pull us, kicking, into life,
breathe spirit into us.

We thank you for the gift in our breath,
the love that we make,
the hope that we cherish,
the grace that encompasses our darkest day.
In smallness and splendor, in storm and serenity,
we celebrate your care and creativity.
We rest in you, as trustingly as any baby.[1]
  —KATHY GALLOWAY

Lectio: Resting in the Word

Begin this exercise by sitting quietly for a few moments, with your eyes open or closed—whichever works best to help you center your thoughts on where you are, rather than on the events of the day. Breathe deeply, and try to let the muscles of your body relax. When you are ready, open with this simple prayer:

> May the words of my mouth, and the meditations of my (our) heart(s) be acceptable to you, O God, my rock and my redeemer. Amen.

1. Read this text through slowly, and simply listen to what it is saying. What is the overall message of this passage? Allow yourself to just absorb the passage in silence for a couple minutes.

O LORD, you have searched me and known me.
You know when I sit down and when I rise up; you discern my thoughts from far away.
You search out my path and my lying down, and are acquainted with all my ways.
Even before a word is on my tongue, O LORD, you know it completely.
You hem me in, behind and before, and lay your hand upon me.
Such knowledge is too wonderful for me; it is so high that I cannot attain it.

Where can I go from your spirit? Or where can I flee
from your presence?
For it was you who formed my inward parts; you knit me
together in my mother's womb.
I praise you, for I am fearfully and wonderfully made.
Wonderful are your works; that I know very well.
My frame was not hidden from you, when I was being
made in secret, intricately woven in the depths of the
earth.
Your eyes beheld my unformed substance. In your book
were written all the days that were formed for me, when
none of them as yet existed.
How weighty to me are your thoughts, O God! How vast
is the sum of them!
I try to count them—they are more than the sand; I come
to the end—I am still with you.
　　—PSALM 139:1–7, 13–18

2.　Read the passage a second time. As you do, listen for a
word or phrase that seems to be an instruction for you.
Is there something that jumps out at you from the text
that feels like God's instruction or guidance for your
life? Make a note of that word or phrase, if you wish,
and quietly contemplate that instruction for a few minutes before moving on.

3.　Read the passage a third time. When you hear the passage you focused on in the second reading, allow
yourself to experience a sense of gratitude for God's

guidance in the word or words that stood out to you. Rest in that sense of thankfulness for a few minutes.

4. Read the passage a fourth time. Do you hear a word or phrase that calls you to confession? Notice what you are feeling at this time, and respond to God as appropriate.

5. Read the passage for the final time, and listen for an overall sense of guidance in the text. Find an image in your mind or in the words themselves that allows you to rest in God's guidance, even if you are not sure what God is asking of you.

If you are doing this exercise by yourself, you may wish to take a few minutes at the end of it and make some notes about your experiences and feelings while doing this. If you are doing this exercise with others, the group may find it helpful to allow some time for those who wish to share their thoughts and feelings.

EPILOGUE

The Fruit of the Spirit

Small Steps

A certain woman named Lydia, a worshiper of God, was
listening to us; she was from the city of Thyatira and a
dealer in purple cloth. The Lord opened her heart to listen eagerly to what was said by Paul.

—ACTS 16:14

*L*ydia's story in Acts is brief—just a few verses. But hers
is the story of a woman who accepted the gift of a
hearing heart and acted on it. Lydia heard Paul and his followers talking about God outside the gates of her city, and
in listening to them, her heart was opened. She was baptized not long after that, along with all the members of her
household, and then life changed for her. It wasn't a huge
change, just a subtle one.[1]

Lydia's story provides a helpful contrast to the biblical
stories of major life disruptions as a result of discerning
with the heart. Not everyone is called to huge tasks like
those of Moses and the prophets. Lydia was a seller of purple fabrics, a luxury material worn only by royalty. Because
of this, and because she had a household of people to have
baptized, we can surmise that Lydia was probably wealthy.
There's no indication that she gave up her profession or her
wealth after hearing God's word, but we're told that she did

open up her heart and home to provide hospitality and care to Paul and his followers. Some scholars say that she was reduced to the minor role of only providing hospitality rather than having a more prominent position. Others say that there is evidence that Lydia was very prominent, that she not only provided hospitality but also ran a small house church from her home. Either way, Lydia exemplifies someone whose discernment resulted in a subtle shift of focus rather than a radical change of life. Her story may be much closer to the experience of most of us than the dramatic changes in Moses' story.

But that doesn't make Lydia any less courageous than Moses. You never know—when you begin to hear with your heart—whether God will call you to go free the slaves or to provide a place of hospitality for others on the path. And even seemingly small and subtle changes can be major ones. I doubt that Lydia ever felt the same way about her world as she did after God called her. Her outward actions might not have looked very different from her neighbors' perspective, but I suspect that her hospitality felt more like ministry to her and less like the parties of old. And even these small changes can feel huge and earthshaking to the person experiencing them. God may not call us to free the slaves, but being a willing recipient of any call requires courage. There is no such thing, in the end, as a small and insignificant call.

What "small" changes have you made in your own life as a result of God's call to you?

Lord, teach me to seek you, and reveal yourself to me as I seek you. For I cannot seek you unless you first teach me and I cannot find you unless you first reveal yourself to me.
—Ambrose of Milan

DAY 30

Getting the Right Answer

The fruit of the Spirit is love, joy, peace, patience, kindness, generosity, faithfulness, gentleness, and self-control.
—GALATIANS 5:22–23

*I*f it were up to me, I'd give an answer different from the one I'm forced to give. We all want an answer to the question How do I know if I've discerned well and clearly? The standard and truthful response is that you'll never know for sure—not this side of the grave, anyway. The closest you'll get to knowing if you've heard clearly is if the action you take as a result of your discernment brings about what is called the fruit of the Spirit. "The fruit of the Spirit is love, joy, peace, patience, kindness, generosity, faithfulness, gentleness, and self-control," says Galatians 5:22–23. If our activities in the world produce these things, then it is generally thought that we have heard clearly and responded well. All of that, of course, is difficult to measure definitively. I'd rather God handed me a gold star for getting the right answer. I'd even settle for a simple e-mail.

Perhaps another way to think about whether you've discerned well is to ask yourself if, in hindsight, you would have chosen differently than you did. Catholic priest and writer Anthony De Mello tells the story of two brothers who were called by God to give up what they owned and serve humanity. The older brother left his family and the woman he had hoped to marry and went off to serve the poor. While doing that, he got embroiled in the political persecutions of the country and was arrested, falsely accused, tortured, and murdered. The second brother ignored God's call, married, became a prosperous businessman, and occasionally gave some of his resources to charities. When the two brothers died, God's response to each of them was identical. "Well done, good and faithful servant!," God said to each. "You have given me ten talents' worth of service. I shall now give you a billion, billion talents' worth of reward. Enter into the joy of your Lord!"[1]

The older brother could have been very upset that his younger brother had received the same reward he had, but, instead, he was pleased. "Lord," he said, "knowing this as I do, if I were to be born and live my life again, I would still do exactly what I did for you."[2]

As you look back on your own life, are there things you've done that you would do exactly the same if you were called to live your life again? What were the fruits of those events or activities? In all likelihood, those choices you would make again produced some of the fruits named in

Galatians, or you would look on them with regret instead of joy. There's no way to know if the choices you're making today are the result of clear or hazy discernment; only time will help you sense whether your response matched God's hopes and dreams for you.

Look back over your shoulder at your life once in a while. If you like what you see, if it feels like you've done something to make the world a little bit better or been someone whose presence has brightened the world for others, chances are you've heard well with your heart. Pat yourself on the back once in a while and say to yourself what God says to you regularly: "Well done, good and faithful servant."

When you look back over your life, what have been the results of hearing well?

Talk with us, Lord, thyself reveal
While here o'er earth we rove;
Speak to our hearts, and let us feel
The kindling of thy love.
With thee conversing we forget
All time, and toil, and care:
Labour is rest, and pain is sweet
If thou, my God, art there.
Here then, my God, vouchsafe to stay,
And bid my heart rejoice;

My bounding heart shall own thy sway,
And echo to thy voice.
Thou callest me to seek thy face—
'Tis all I wish to seek;
To attend the whispers of thy grace,
And hear thee inly speak.
Let this my every hour employ,
Till I thy glory see,
Enter into my Master's joy,
And find my heaven in thee.
   —CHARLES WESLEY

Benediction

*A*t the end of his famous Rule—his guidebook for living a monastic life—the sixth-century St. Benedict tells us that his Rule is only a beginning, that there is much more to be read and pondered on the road to perfection in the monastic life. So, too, is this book only a starting point. The discerning life is just that—a lifelong endeavor. My hope is that this book has provided you with a semi-legible road map for beginning and continuing on your search for a hearing heart.

Let me leave you with a prayer from my own Anglican tradition that I've found helpful in my own travels:

> Almighty God, to you all hearts are open, all desires known, and from you no secrets are hid: Cleanse the thoughts of our hearts by the inspiration of your Holy Spirit, that we may perfectly love you, and worthily magnify your holy Name; through Christ our Lord. Amen.[1]

Blessings on you as you search for and walk the paths to which God has called you. May God, the Creator, Christ, and the Holy Spirit bless you and keep you forever.

Using This Book in Small Groups

earning to Hear with the Heart can be used with a prayer or spiritual direction group or with a congregational small group that is interested in studying discernment. An outline for a six-week class follows.

First Week

Begin the first class with a few moments of quiet followed by a prayer for God's guidance as the class works on discerning God's will over the next six weeks. Then allow some time for the members of the class to introduce themselves. You might ask them to say something about their reasons for participating in the class and about their hopes and expectations.

Because participants haven't yet begun reading the meditations, spend some time during this first session exploring the topic of discernment. You'll find a great deal of information about that in my other book *Hearing with the Heart: A Gentle Guide to Discerning God's Will for Your*

Life if you need pointers or suggestions. It can be helpful to ask participants what their perception of discernment is—in advance of reading about it—and surface preconceptions or the variety of ideas in the room.

Near the end of your time together explain the structure of the rest of the course or workshop. It is helpful, although not imperative, for class members to focus on one issue or concern in their life that would benefit from discernment over the next weeks. Invite them to consider that and read the meditations with their concern in mind. Ask participants to spend some time reading the meditation for each day over the next four weeks and consider the question that closes each meditation. If the participants like, they can record those thoughts in a journal. Provide some time for them to explore what they have discovered each week, beginning with week two. But remind everyone that confidentiality is important. Anything discussed in class, any confidences or stories shared, should not be repeated outside of the group. Allow some time for questions at the end of your time together, and ask participants to read the introduction to this book, along with the first week's meditations for next week's class. Close with a prayer.

Second Week Through the Fifth

Begin each class with a time of silence and a prayer. Take some time to debrief about what people discovered that week as they read the meditations and pondered them. If the group is a large one, it may be helpful to do this in small groups so everyone who wants to share some insights has the opportunity to do so.

After people have had some time to talk about their discoveries during the week, use the lectio exercise— "Resting in the Word"—that's provided for each week. Before the exercise begins, ask for five different volunteers to read the passage aloud. Begin with a few minutes of silence so the group can get quiet and focused, and then read the question or instruction for the first reading, and then ask the first volunteer to read the passage. Instruct the group to maintain silence between readings, and let them know you'll break the silence with the question that frames the next reading. Ask one volunteer to read the passage after you've spoken the question out loud. At the end of all five readings, allow some time to discuss people's insights either in the group as a whole or in small groups, depending on the size of the class.

Close each session with a few more minutes of silence, followed by a prayer.

At the end of the fifth week's session, invite participants to read the final two meditations in the book sometime during the coming week and spend some time journaling or reflecting on their experiences with discernment over the past five weeks.

Sixth Week

Begin the class with centering silence and prayer as you did in the previous weeks. Then ask participants to share their reflections about their conversations with God from the past weeks. This can be done in large or small groups as needed. If you use small groups, it may be helpful to invite everyone back together to share overall insights with the whole group before the class ends.

Close the class with either a time of silence followed by prayer, or a brief worship service of your choice. *Hearing with the Heart* contains a worship service that is focused specifically on discernment, for those who would like one.

Notes

Introduction

1. Robert Fulghum, *Everything I Need to Know I Learned in Kindergarten: Uncommon Thoughts on Common Things* (New York: Villard Books, 1988), pp. 16–17.
2. Quoted in Edward C. Sellner, *The Celtic Soul Friend: A Trusted Guide for Today* (Notre Dame, Ind.: Ave Maria Press, 2002), p. 4.

Day 1: Ask the Right Question

1. Rainer Maria Rilke, *Letters to a Young Poet* (New York: Norton: 1934), p. 35.

Day 3: Follow Your Own Path

1. Anthony De Mello, *The Song of the Bird* (New York: Doubleday, 1982), p. 79.
2. Anthony De Mello (1982), p. 79.
3. John Anthony McGuckin, trans., *The Book of Mystical Chapters: Meditations on the Soul's Ascent from the Desert Fathers and Other Early Christian Contemplatives* (Boston: Shambhala, 2002), pp. 15–16.

Day 5: Is Your Prayer Too Small?

1. I am indebted to Dr. Joseph Driskill for teaching me this exercise.

Day 7: Keep an Open and Hearing Heart

1. Edward Hays, *The Ladder* (Leavenworth, Kans.: Forest of Peace Publishing, 1999), pp. 54–56.

Day 8: Pay Attention, Listen, and Learn

1. Diane Schoemperlen, *Our Lady of the Lost and Found: A Novel of Mary, Faith, and Friendship* (New York: Viking, 2001), p. 1.

Day 11: Listen to Your Body

1. Gloria Hutchinson, *A Retreat with Gerald Manley Hopkins and Hildegard of Bingen* (Cincinnati, Ohio: St. Anthony Messenger Press, 1995), p. 12.

Day 13: Holiness in the Oddest Places

1. Robert Fulghum, *All I Really Need to Know I Learned in Kindergarten: Uncommon Thoughts on Common Things* (New York: Villard Books, 1986), p. 166.

2. David Adam, *Tides and Seasons: Modern Prayers in the Celtic Tradition* (London: SPCK, 1989), p. 13.

Day 14: Quiet the Hamsters

1. Anonymous, *The Rule of Taizé* (New York: Seabury Press, 1968), p. 53.

2. David Adam, *Tides and Seasons: Modern Prayers in the Celtic Tradition* (London: SPCK, 1989), p. 90.

Lectio: Resting in the Word

1. Anonymous, *The Rule of the Society of Saint John the Evangelist* (Boston: Cowley Publications, 1977), p. 47.

Day 15: Pockets of Trust and Surrender

1. Anne Lamott, *Traveling Mercies: Some Thoughts on Faith* (New York: Pantheon Books, 1999), p. 179.

2. Anne Lamott (1999), p. 180.

3. Anne Lamott, p. 180.

Day 17: Consult the Truth Tellers

1. Anthony de Mello, *Taking Flight: A Book of Story Meditations* (New York: Image Books, 1988), p. 180.

Day 18: Experience and Discernment

1. T. H. White, *The Once and Future King* (New York: Ace Books, 1939), p. 46.
2. T. H. White (1939), p. 51.
3. Edward Hays, *The Ladder* (Leavenworth, Kans.: Forest of Peace Books, 1999), p. 94.
4. Edward Hays (1999), p. 94.
5. Edward Hays, p. 95.

Day 19: Examining the Heart

1. Frederick Buechner, *Telling Secrets: A Memoir* (New York: HarperSanFrancisco, 1991), p. 3.

Day 20: The Blessing of Friends

1. Benedicta Ward, *The Sayings of the Desert Fathers* (Kalamazoo, Mich.: Cistercian Publications, 1975) p. 222.

Day 21: Wise Guides

1. Edward Hays, *Prayers for the Domestic Church* (Easton, Kans.: Forest of Peace Books, 1979), p. 66.

Day 22: Just Keep Trying

1. Brother Lawrence of the Resurrection, trans. John J. Delaney, *The Practice of the Presence of God* (New York: Image Books, 1977), p. 47.
2. Thich Nhat Hanh, *Anger: Wisdom for Cooling the Flames* (New York: Riverhead Books, 2001), p. 18.
3. Brother Lawrence, p. 40.

Day 23: Play and Pray

1. Sue Woodruff, *Meditations with Mechtild of Magdeburg* (Santa Fe, N.M.: Bear & Company, 1982), p. 47.
2. Sue Woodruff (1982), p. 48.
3. Sue Woodruff, p. 50.

Day 24: Discernment When God Is AWOL
1.   Richard J. Foster, *Prayers from the Heart* (San Francisco: HarperSanFrancisco, 1994), pp. 6–7.

Day 25: A Little Reason, a Little Imagination
1.   Horton Davies, ed., *The Communion of Saints: Prayers of the Famous* (Grand Rapids, Mich.: Eerdmans, 1990), p. 33.

Day 28: This Is Your Life
1.   Kathy Galloway, ed., *The Pattern of Our Days: Worship in the Celtic Tradition from the Iona Community* (Mahwah, N.J.: Paulist Press, 1996), pp. 128–129.

Day 29: Small Steps
1.   I am grateful to Gerrit Scott Dawson for this insight found in his chapter, "Radical Availability," in *Companions in Christ: A Small-Group Experience in Spiritual Formation, Participant's Book* (Nashville, Tenn.: Upper Room Books, 2001), p. 185.

Day 30: Getting the Right Answer
1.   Anthony De Mello, *The Song of the Bird* (New York: Image Books, 1982), p. 118.
2.   Anthony De Mello (1982), p. 118.

Benediction
1.   *The Book of Common Prayer*, p. 355.

The Author

Debra K. Farrington is a wise writer, popular retreat leader, and publishing insider with a growing following. She is the publisher of Morehouse Publishing. She was manager of the Graduate Theological Union Bookstore in Berkeley, California, and has published in *Spirituality and Health, Catholic Digest, The Lutheran, U.S. Catholic, Publishers Weekly,* and many other magazines and journals. This is her sixth book. Debra's website is www.debrafarrington.com.

Other Books of Interest

Hearing with the Heart

A Gentle Guide to Discerning God's Will for Your Life

Debra K. Farrington

$19.95 Cloth

ISBN: 0-7879-5959-6

What does God wish for you in your life? How do you listen for God's gracious guidance as you face daily decisions, both big and small? And how do you know that what you are hearing comes from God and not your ego or simply your own wishful thinking?

Only through learning to hear with our hearts tuned closely to God can we discern how we should find our way through the crowded and confusing thickets of our lives. In *Hearing with the Heart,* popular writer and retreat leader Debra Farrington leads you through a gentle process for discovering how to invite God's presence into every aspect of your daily life. Her story-filled discussions of key practices such as prayer, meditation, reading and reflection, and attentiveness to your body, your studies, and your relationships with your friends and family, help you discover how to be open to discerning God's will. Filled with a wealth of exercises, guidelines, and tools, *Hearing with the Heart* gives you the practical help you need to bring you closer to God. As you put these suggestions into practice you will find yourself opening more and more to God's infinite possibilities for you.

Hearing with the Heart samples a broad range of stories taken from the Bible, classic and contemporary literature, and everyday experiences. It can be an indispensable resource for discerning how to proceed at major crossroads and navigate life's challenges at work, in relationships, or during crisis situations and how to truly be partners with God in creating your life. This gentle and compassionate companion for helping to reveal God's hopes and desires for you will not only bring joy to your life but also to the lives of others and to a world where peace, love, and charity can flourish.

DEBRA K. FARRINGTON—an insightful writer and popular retreat leader—is publisher of Morehouse Publishing and the former manager of the Graduate Theological Union Bookstore in Berkeley, California. Farrington has written for a wide variety of publications including *Spirituality and Health, Catholic Digest, The Lutheran, Publishers Weekly, U.S. Catholic,* and many others.

[Price subject to change]